Peter was born in the late 1920's, educated at the local village school and later Ripon Grammar School. From an early age he showed an aptitude for after school activities rather than the daytime ones, and has since maintained he could create more with a hammer and nails than with pen and ink.

Always keen on sport, he did well at cricket and probably could have followed a football career having two offers of trials by football league clubs. Not too keen on a strict training regime, these were turned down in favour of playing for fun.

A country upbringing meant nature was all around and he has always had a healthy interest in all its aspects. When time and money allowed a decent camera, it gave the opportunity to film much of the wildlife around and created another hobby. It has since been valuable in helping to record events in the latter half of his career.

FROM PETS TO PUMAS

Peter A Wait

From Pets To Pumas

Best wishes
Peter A. Wait.

Vanguard Press

VANGUARD PAPERBACK

© Copyright 2006
Peter A Wait

The right of Peter A Wait to be identified as author of
this work has been asserted by him in accordance with the
Copyright, Designs and Patents Act 1988

All Rights Reserved

No reproduction, copy or transmission of this publication
may be made without written permission.
No paragraph of this publication may be reproduced,
copied or transmitted save with the written permission of the
publisher, or in accordance with the provisions
of the Copyright Act 1956 (as amended).

Any person who does any unauthorised act in relation to
this publication may be liable to criminal
prosecution and civil claims for damage.

**Photograph credits
by courtesy of the late John Doidge**

A CIP catalogue record for this title is
available from the British Library

ISBN 1 84386 240 9

*Vanguard Press is an imprint of
Pegasus Elliot MacKenzie Publishers Ltd.*
www.pegasuspublishers.com

First Published in 2006

**Vanguard Press
Sheraton House Castle Park
Cambridge England**

Printed & Bound in Great Britain

This book is dedicated to my wife, Maveen, who has put up with me, my peculiarities and a penchant for bringing my work and animals home, for nigh on fifty years. Given the opportunity to live my life again, I do not and would not change a thing, though maybe I would not mind being twenty again and know what I know now.

A story of how a boy's love of animals and his many pets eventually led to a career in a leading zoo. Starting life on a Yorkshire farm, where he spent his youth, he became a farm manager for fifteen years, followed by almost twenty five with the North of England Zoological Society at Chester, where he was curator.

Some of the views expressed are the author's personal opinions and not necessarily those shared by the management of the zoo.

It was two o'clock in the morning on a mild July night and I was alone with two of my friends. On this occasion it was Sheba, a twenty year old Asian Elephant, and her newly born calf Mottie, named after Mr George Mottershead, O.B.E., the founder director of Chester Zoo.

Mottie was something rather special. According to all the experts he should not have been conceived, let alone be present here in the flesh. His father was an African bull elephant, called Jumbolina, the only African elephant in the collection at that time. This, and having an Asian elephant as his mother, made him, to my knowledge, the only hybrid ever seen, and probably never to be seen again.

He was born in July 1978, just over a year after Jubilee was bred in the zoo, he being the first elephant to be born and reared in Britain. I looked on Jubilee as another friend, and he became a celebrity in his own right, receiving as many as 3840 cards from his many friends and admirers from all over the world on his third birthday.

Unfortunately Mottie was not as robust as Jubilee, and he needed constant attention, which was the reason I was there at that unearthly hour, …Apart from the two animals, I was alone with my thoughts.

My story starts just fifty years earlier.

Chapter 1

The Early Years

I was born on a small farm in Yorkshire, and therefore it was not surprising that I would develop an early interest in the animal world. My father's farm at that time bordered the River Ure, being appropriately called River House, and it was there I spent the first few years of my life.

It was a stock farm, holding all the usual kinds of domestic animals such as dairy cows, at that time shorthorns, sheep, pigs, poultry and horses together with the usual array of dogs, cats and some pigeons. Horses did the heavy work on the farm and they were also used for transport, pulling a selection of traps, carts and wagons. Cars then were few and far between, and life went on at a leisurely pace.

The Ure was a river prone to flooding, and following heavy rain or melting snow higher up the dale, much of the lower lying land would be covered with water, at times coming up to the house itself, and sometimes filling the cellar. It was after one such spate that I received my first lesson in feeding animals. As the flood subsided it left behind pools in the hollows, which were excellent places for small boys to investigate. Quite often, some fish get left behind and on this particular occasion a small friend and I spotted a shoal of small eels. With the aid of wellingtons, which soon proved totally inadequate, and a net, it wasn't long before we had caught half a bucket full. The wriggling mass seemed to excite our flock of Aylesbury ducks which, up to that moment, hadn't succeeded in catching any. We started to feed the ducks with the contents of the bucket, and the resulting noise brought father to see what was going on. Some of the eels were visibly wriggling inside the ducks crops. He then seemed to get rather more excited than the ducks, and in a voice a little louder than normal said, *"Hey don't do that, you will choke the b... things."* Fortunately for us they didn't, and the ducks became friends.

Because of the presence of foxes and the danger of predation, the ducks had to be fastened up each evening, and this became one of my daily tasks for which I was suitably rewarded with pocket money each Saturday. The ducks soon learnt the routine and usually came first call and usually from the direction of the river, knowing once they reached the farm and shelter there would be food waiting for them. As they came home, on reaching a certain point in the field, they would form a column which was then strictly adhered to until they were safely fastened up in their shed. I soon realised I could cash in on this situation when visitors were around. They usually stood amazed at the ducks reaction to my sergeant major like command to sort themselves out and get into line, something they would have done even if I had told them not to.

It was soon after this that father was given the opportunity of acquiring another farm about two miles away. This holding had a larger acreage, with arable as well as meadow, giving more scope to care for a growing family which included an elder sister. It was here I spent the next twenty years of my life.

Although there were all the usual animals associated with a farm, pets were not frowned upon, and I never seemed to be without some of one sort or another.

One of the first I remember was a black and white Dutch rabbit which appeared when I was about six years old. I do not recall from where it came, but like many small boys, I'm afraid I did not look after it as well as I should have, and relied on father to feed it when I forgot. One morning came the ultimatum, *"If you are not going to feed it I will let it go in the wood."* I was determined not to let this happen, and said I would find another home for it amongst my friends. One day a few weeks later, I returned home from school and told mother I had sold my rabbit. *"How much did you sell it for?"* she asked. *"Four pence,"* says I. *"Well I will give you the money because your father has let it go,"* she said. In true Yorkshire fashion I suggested it was worth sixpence, and needless to say that is what I got. I then spent a few hours searching the wood for the rabbit hoping to collect another four pence, but the search was fruitless. I had a sneaky suspicion that dad had either sold it himself or given it away.

One of my uncles, a butcher by trade, kept budgerigars as a hobby, and on my seventh birthday gave me a pair of his birds. The cock bird was a brilliant blue and the hen green. I will always remember her and her incredibly sharp beak with which she seemed to take delight in trying it out on my fingers at every opportunity. I had great expectations from the budgerigars, thinking they would be talking to me in no time at all, and was rather disappointed when all I got was an incessant chatter in their own language. Though somewhat disillusioned in their vocal efforts, I found them to be well educated in other matters, as by the end of the summer they had produced two broods and I had a total of ten budgerigars. As my parents had been inveigled into buying the seed for the enterprise, it became a nice little earner, but my enthusiasm was rather dampened when one of the farm cats made off with the hen bird. My one wish was that the bird had bitten the cat as hard as it had bitten me on numerous occasions before it perished so prematurely.

It was about this time that my sister introduced me to guinea pigs. She was the proud possessor of a large hen hut which in today's terms may well be classed as an oversized Wendy House, and was grandly called Ramsbottom Mansion. This was a forbidden area, for me, only her and her close friends were allowed to use the facilities, but now and then my close friends and I were invited to try out their experimental cooking. Potatoes baked in an open fire were just about acceptable even though their skins were burnt black, and without doubt would have been turned down if presented at the dining table and would have been looked upon in absolute horror by today's clean food fanatics. However, none of the outdoor *'meals'* seemed to have any adverse effect on the victims and probably bore out one of Grandmothers expressions, that everybody should eat *'a peck of muck'*.

My sister had been given a white guinea pig, and this in turn had been given a cage in the *'mansion'* and answered to the name of Betsy Ramsbottom, When I was introduced to the animal, it's whistling call when approached rather appealed to me and I thought I would have one or two. A few enquiries at school soon located a trio that had outstayed their welcome, and I was the new owner of three free guinea pigs. A cage wasn't needed as father told me their whistling frightened rats and I could put them in an empty granary for the time being. Previous enquiries soon yielded others, and a little lack of enthusiasm on my part in paying for them, meant I now had eight of various sex and size for no outlay. Early the following year, threshing corn meant that the granary was required to store the grain. Father's excursion to see its suitability was followed by an exasperated outburst that he had counted forty-five of the things and that they must be eating as much as the bacon pigs. Within a day or two a solution had been found which meant they all went to a research establishment at twelve pence a head and five pounds went into the kitty. Unfortunately, I had to spring clean the granary before the money was finally mine. I am not sure about the theory of the whistling keeping rats away, but certainly they were not seen whilst the guinea pigs were in residence, but soon appeared when the corn replaced them.

I was eleven years old and had just stated a new education period at the local grammar school when the war started in 1939. Part of the farm was commandeered by the military for an army camp and temporary barracks were built on one of the fields. The camp, became an interesting place for me, having searchlights, artillery and tracked vehicles, but I soon came to the conclusion the camp kitchens had more to offer.

By now I had an eye for the more material things in life, for which purchasing power was required. This tempted me back into the rabbit business; these I had already decided could be fed with waste from the camp kitchen. I scoured the countryside on my bicycle, buying as many rabbits as I could find, and as cheaply as I could. The best were kept for breeding stock and the rest I sold to the officers mess at the camp, and also to a local RAF officers mess at fifty pence a time to supplement their rations. This arrangement became quite lucrative for me, as the camp was supplying most of the food for the rabbits as well as buying the rabbits from me to augment their diet. However, they appeared to be quite happy with the deal and I certainly was. Soldiers came and soldiers went, but fortunately, others were always ready to continue the with rabbit enterprise and kept me in pocket money for most of the years at war.

Goat, Squeak, and kid with dog Judy and father.

The next venture concerned goats. A gentleman in the next village had a large black and tan nanny which I had seen many times tethered on the side of the road during my cycling trips. He stopped me one day and asked me if I would like to have the animal, as apparently it kept getting loose in his garden and disposing of anything, that was edible, which I found out later, hardly leaves anything as nothing seems inedible to a goat. I jumped at this opportunity without a second thought. *'Owt for nowt,'* as the Yorkshire saying goes, always appealed to me and besides I had heard father talking about goats and gathered from conversations that they ate all the rubbish other animals left. They also had some mysterious quality that stopped cows aborting their calves, so I thought he would be pleased to see this addition to the farm stock.

Well he did seem enthusiastic when I told him of the acquisition, but I was not at all sure that he had realised the full potential of this particular goat. Squeak, as I had decided to call her, first had to be brought home. There were transport difficulties at the time with the petrol rationing, but life was much more leisurely and time did not seem to matter so much, so I decided Squeak could walk home. A four mile walk with a goat on a piece of string didn't seem much of a challenge, or very far when I set off on the journey home with her, well secured on a short lead. However she was far more interested in the roadside herbage than keeping up with me, so it became a battle of will power, with her easily the winner. The situation changed somewhat when she had eaten her fill, but then she wanted to go in the opposite direction to me, and after about three hours, I was extremely pleased to see dad with the family car looking for us. In this time the two of us had managed to cover less than half the distance, and Squeak was by far the freshest. The next problem faced was to get a very uncooperative goat into the back of a Ford 8 car, and finally having accomplished that, keep it under control for the rest of the journey. Before we reached that destination, however, she decided to vacate all the vegetation she had eaten in the first half of the trip. Goats do not appear to smell too badly in the open air, but in the confines of a small car it did become a little unbearable to say the least, and despite various perfumed washes, the car reeked for weeks.

Although I had a tether for Squeak which restricted her wanderings to a twenty yard circle, she was seldom confined to it, and was allowed to wander at will. Most of the family soon remembered to keep the garden gate closed; otherwise things had a habit of disappearing. She wasn't averse to showing her displeasure to anybody who annoyed her, or upset her routine in any way, by lowering her head and charging in their direction at full tilt. To her cost, Mother roused her temper when she found the goat interfering with the week's washing one day. Deciding enough was enough she took the offending animal into the field and put her on the tether, only to spend the rest of the day wishing she hadn't, as it was never safe to turn your back on Squeak when she was in a bad mood. A few weeks later it became apparent that she had shared her accommodation with a billy goat before I had acquired her, something that wasn't mentioned at the time, and I soon became the owner of another two goats, one male, one female. Squeak and her offspring got me into all sorts of trouble, and we had already learnt they don't eat the rubbish left by other animals if there is anything better. If they were not in the barn eating cattle food or pulling hay from the stacks, they were in the kitchen garden chewing some delicacy or other. Clean washing hung on the line still seemed to have some peculiar fascination. Her biggest crime however, happened when her and her erstwhile young, found their way into the army camp kitchen after a baking session, and sampled the freshly baked bread loaves on display. Not satisfied with clearing up one loaf, they sampled each in turn by taking a bite from every one within reach, and compounded the crime by leaving vast amounts of calling cards. The camp baker was not a happy man, but had to admit he was responsible for leaving the door open, and the place unattended, and previously encouraging the goats with titbits. By this time the goats had become firm favourites with the troops, who suffering from the boredom of camp life had more or less adopted them as unofficial company mascots, which was further cemented in an incident concerning a sergeant and Squeak's hard head. This was a situation totally acceptable to the goats, who only saw it as another source of food.

The goats were still part of the farm's furniture when the donkeys made an appearance. As it happened, I was at Boroughbridge auction market with father when a pen of these animals took my eye. I overhead somebody say they were a batch of seaside donkeys, for which at that time, there was no work on the beach. I persuaded father to let me bid for one as they came into the ring. He did not seem particularly impressed with the idea, but knowing I did not have much cash at the time, obviously thought it unlikely I would be successful. As they went through the ring one by one, I was beginning to despair, as my total commitment was three pounds and fifty pence, and the donkeys were selling at five to ten pounds each. Then into the ring came an elderly looking female with a small foal running behind. She appeared to have been rolling in something nasty and her front hooves were badly overgrown but that did not worry me because nobody seemed really interested in the pair. They were almost knocked down to me for two pounds and following another two half-hearted bids, were mine for four pounds. I then had to borrow fifty pence from my cousin, who had come with us for the ride, to pay my debts. I think afterwards he regretted ever getting involved with me and my donkeys, and come to think of it, I don't believe he ever got his fifty pence back.

Having acquired the two donkeys I then had to get them home. Father said paying for transport was out of the question, and as he had walked cattle to and fro from the market many a time, we could walk the donkey's home. My cousin was seconded to help as he was considered part of the conspiracy to buy them. The donkeys however, proved far more tractable than the goat, and it wasn't long before we were heading for home, me leading the female, and my cousin following behind, making certain the foal didn't stray too far. I am sure they were pleased to get away from the noise of the market into the peace and quiet of the country lanes.

Unfortunately, we were soon treated to the vagaries of the English weather. After travelling less than a mile of the six ahead of us, the heavens opened and we were soaked to the skin within minutes, this continued in similar vein all the way home. Even allowing for the fact that donkeys were a rare sight in our part of the world, we were hardly prepared for the remarks passed in our direction. Some came possibly out of sympathy for our bedraggled looks but in the main were more derogatory and certainly not very amusing to us at the time, though admittedly we must have looked a comical sight dripping water at every stride, and beginning to show signs of weariness. One dear old lady asked if we were going to Bethlehem, offering to point us in the right direction, although I declined to ask which of us reminded her of Joseph and which was Mary. In fact I was rather pleased as darkness came and we were not quite so conspicuous. It took about three hours before we finally trudged into the farmyard like a pair of drowned rats, only to be greeted with howls of laughter from the assembled family who had obviously been watching for our arrival from the comfort of the kitchen window. A loose box on the farm had been prepared in readiness for the donkeys, and although I think they were less tired than we were, they were not sorry to get off the road and tuck into the waiting food. After they were safely put to bed it was our turn for some dry clothes and a warm tea, both of which were truly appreciated, and I thought well deserved, even though nobody else mentioned it.

Jenny and Jack, as they were subsequently called, proved to be one of my better buys, as after a couple of visits to the blacksmith (the charges being conveniently put on father's account), Jenny's hooves were returned almost to normal. The blacksmith also enjoyed the experience, being local tradesman he said he had turned his hand to many jobs, but this was something completely new to him, working on a donkey's feet.

Jenny the donkey with maternal grandfather and young cousin, approx: 1942.

My maternal grandfather, who had been a carpenter prior to retiring and was now living with us, built a small cart using an old car axle and cut down shafts from an old pony cart. I painted it yellow and red, the same colours (and the same paint) as used on the farm carts. Some pony harness scrounged from a neighbour was adapted for Jenny, and it was with a little apprehension, that harness, donkey and cart were all put together. The worry was misplaced as everything went perfectly, and I felt certain Jenny must have had past experience pulling a cart because she seemed to know exactly what to do, even in reverse. We three became a regular sight in the area, three because it was almost impossible to leave Jack behind, as wherever Jenny went, he had to follow. The only way it could be achieved was to fasten him up in the stable, but then he would bray non-stop until reunited with his mother, a noise not appreciated by anyone within earshot. I never really managed to break him from this habit, or to get him to pull the cart, in fact one of the times I tried him in the harness he lay down and managed to break both shafts of the cart. Jenny however, was a real worker and came in handy for many light jobs around the farm, and visiting friends in the district. She was never in a hurry to go away from home, but once heading back, she could be relied upon to get you home at a trot and sometimes even break into a gallop. An added advantage in this mode of transport was that I didn't have to pedal uphill. As Jack matured, he would tolerate me riding him, but resist the efforts of anyone else. I could safely challenge anybody to ride him knowing they would be unceremoniously dumped within seconds of getting on his back; otherwise he would just lie down and roll over. I found the best ride could be obtained by physically restraining him at one end of the field and getting a friend to take Jenny to the other, and once given the opportunity to get together he would go at full gallop until reunited. Unfortunately using this method meant we didn't always arrive together, as he would try various devious ways of getting rid of his load during the trip, but anyone who has ridden a donkey at full gallop would probably agree that a good walk is better anyway.

The donkeys remained a fixture on the farm for many years, well after I left home and until Jenny succumbed to old age, which Jack appeared to accept, and then he found solace with a retired racehorse owned by a neighbour. He was given on a permanent loan basis, the pair becoming inseparable companions, living out their lives together.

It was also early in the war years when I made the acquaintance of a young owl. I was on my way home from school and getting close to our drive, when I noticed what appeared to be a bundle of brown paper under the hedge. When the object moved, closer inspection revealed it was a forlorn looking tawny owl chick which somehow had been prematurely ejected from its nest. Its downy plumage and wet and bedraggled appearance, showed it was not ready to face the world without some help. I decided there and then to take it, not really considering at the time how I was going to feed him. As I attempted to pick him up (I assumed it to be a male without any knowledge of its sex), he fell over backwards and stuck the talons of both feet into my hands. Not deterred by this action, I stuffed him down inside my jacket and continued on my way.

Ollie, as I christened him, developed into a great character and was arguably my favourite bird. I supposed all owls fed on mice, so they became the bulk of his diet, being caught in half a dozen little nipper traps placed around the farm in strategic places such as corn bins. I kept Ollie in a granary on the farm, where he developed rapidly and was soon flying strongly. He also became less dependent on me for food and was obviously predating on the farm rodent population which was attracted to the corn in the granary. Ollie would fly straight to my shoulder when I approached, and would be quite happy to sit there while I was wandering about outside with him. He also developed a not so endearing habit of biting hard on my ear when I was least expecting it, which eventually lost him his favourite perch. He was later allowed the freedom of the farm and stayed around for a number of years and never showed any fear of human presence. I would like to think that other tawny owls that appeared afterwards were direct descendants of him (or her) because I never knew for sure.

Jack (another one) came a couple of years later. He was a young jackdaw that came down a chimney in a nearby house, and I was asked by the lady occupant, if I would go and remove it, getting the impression that any way would be acceptable, with no questions asked. When I arrived, I assumed it had come from a nest in the chimney as it was not fully developed, but even so, capable of short flights. It was incredible how something so small could make such a mess – soot was everywhere, even on the ceiling, and I am afraid I added to the confusion in my attempts to catch it. When I finally got the situation under control and the bird was in my hands, it looked so pathetic that I hadn't the heart to do anything else but take it home. He was given the name, Jack, because that was what he appeared to say whenever he was hungry. He had an amazing insatiable appetite and would eat almost anything edible, but also had rather unclean habits, and was therefore totally banned from the house. He became such a character it was impossible not to like him, though many times he came within an inch of him getting his neck rung. One of his self-taught party tricks was to wait until the washing was on the line then walk the full length of it, pulling out the pegs en route, many of which were taken away to a secret hiding place. He was attracted to anything of a bright colour, and if that too was light enough to carry away, it would also disappear. I always hoped to discover his hoard in the hope he had discovered something valuable to secrete. Another trick up his sleeve was to swoop down on my father from some convenient perch, knocking the trilby he always wore, from his head in the process. This seemed to amuse Jack and anybody else who saw it happen, but not father, who constantly threatened to *'shoot that b... bird'*. Fortunately for Jack that never happened, and he eventually flew off with the almost resident flock of other jackdaws. I did however see him again on numerous occasions, flying around, as he was instantly recognisable by his distinctive call, but I think I can honestly say, not missed by the majority of people who he had come into contact with, since his unfortunate first flight down the chimney.

During the war years, I also had ferrets, which was a project fully supported by grandfather who, being a keen sportsman, enjoyed all the country pursuits, and which of course meant I could rely on him to help subsidise the venture. Pest control on the farm then was important, and ferreting was one of the best means of controlling rabbits as well as a good way of supplementing the meat ration, and any surplus, a means of supplementing my pocket money.

My two favourite ferrets were the first two I had, called Queenie and Oscar. I bought Queenie from a local gamekeeper for fifty pence, borrowed from grandfather. She was a small white female, not much larger than a weasel and equally as active as one, and so adept at bolting rabbits, you had to be quick to get the nets down to catch them as they shot out of the holes. I thought I had lost her once when she disappeared down a two-inch drainpipe, but somehow she managed to turn round inside and reappear seconds later when she realised that the mission was fruitless.

I found Oscar when out ferreting with grandfather, and

he had obviously been lost by others with the same intention as us, and left to his own devices. He was covered in white bumps, which I mentioned to grandfather, who informed me they were not bumps but ticks, probably gathered whilst sleeping in the rabbit burrows during the time he was at liberty. A dressing of louse powder we had for the cattle seemed to kill them all off, but then each had to be removed afterwards with a pair of tweezers as their heads were buried in the skin, an operation not fully appreciated by Oscar who made his displeasure known. He turned out to be a massive polecat, just the opposite in disposition to Queenie, as he wouldn't expend any more energy than was necessary. Show him a rabbit hole however, and one sniff was all that was needed. If he shook himself and started chattering you could be certain there were rabbits at home, if he turned away showing no interest, you could safely go on to the next burrow. He was strong enough to physically pull a rabbit out the burrow should it not bolt, a feat that he frequently did. The pair bred annually, producing offspring of both colours, and I never experienced any difficulties in finding homes for them. When one of them got out and made a foray round the army camp, it caused quite an argument, but few of the troops got close to identifying the species. I heard later that it had been called most things between a hedgehog and an otter.

Maternal grandfather, father and cousin after a successful rabbiting, during war years 1943.

I also well remember the day when setting off with father and grandfather and looking forward to a morning's ferreting, the three of us plus equipment, were in the little cart pulled by Jenny with Jack and Grandfather's Labrador, Bess, trotting behind. We were making our way to a large rabbit warren in a sand hill on the farm when suddenly, halfway across the field, a passing crow scored a direct bulls eye on the back of grandfather's hand, which was holding the reins at the time. *"Don't wipe it off, it's lucky,"* said father. The indignant reply came in very explicit terms, which I wouldn't dream of repeating here, but roughly translated meant father was mistaken if he thought that he was going to spend the day with a hand that looked as if it had been dipped in whitewash.

I considered Oscar and Queenie the best two ferrets I had seen, when working in tandem, even if my judgement was somewhat biased, and others that followed never appeared to match their qualities. Even so, think that ferrets are a very misunderstood and underrated species which could be kept more often as an intelligent domestic pet.

All these unforgettable animals had a share in my life and in their way did their bit to help me appreciate my country upbringing. They also gave me the opportunity to begin to understand the complicated world of nature and probably wetted my appetite for the career I was eventually to follow.

Chapter 2

Some of My Best Friends were Dogs

Dogs have frequently been described as man's best friend and I would agree whole-heartedly with that statement. I have never been without a dog for a companion and friend except for about a year, when making a career move from looking after domestic stock to caring for exotic animals, and would without doubt recommend them as the most rewarding, faithful and uncomplaining pet one could have. Having said that, I would go a little further and say two are better than one, as being a pack animal, they are company for each other and more apt to show their true colours.

All the dogs I have owned or been concerned with have had memorable attributes and some of them and thoroughly unforgettable.

Grandad Wait, Peter & sister on knees, two cousins and Roy the dog. August 1928.

My first companion was around when I was too young to appreciate him, but tales of him as a guardian to me as a baby, have been spoken of many times. Old Roy was really my paternal grandfather's dog and lived across the road from River House. He was a large, shaggy sheepdog spending more time with us than at home. I am told he immediately took a shine to the new baby in the family and would howl dejectedly if I cried. When I was outside in the pram, he was so protective, nothing was allowed to approach within yards, be it hen, cat or cattle. Strangers too were not tolerated, and it was only the people he knew intimately that were able to get anywhere near his pup.

Roy was around when I started to walk and was instrumental in helping me to find my feet. Apparently, I would get two handfuls of his long hair to help me to my feet, and then he would persuade my legs to follow. Later he would take me for walks rather than the other way round and I could usually be found, just by calling the dog.

Father used to delight in telling the story of the captive postman which also concerned Roy. In the late 1920's doors were seldom locked nor was it necessary to do so, and back doors were the ones used by most visitors, the front doors only being used occasionally on most farms.

It was the postman's habit to go round to the back door, knock, walk in and leave the post on the kitchen table, and on this particular day an early shopping expedition meant the house was empty when the postman called. Roy must have seen him making the usual visit and when he turned to leave via the door, Roy was there with teeth bared.

Afterwards, the postman said, *"I would not have gone past even if I had been offered a fortune, the warning was so obvious. I thought, I will give him a few minutes and he will tire and go away. I looked out about five minutes later, but he was still there growling. I then had a brainwave – I would go out of the front door. A quick glance reassured me he was still at the back door waiting for me to come out, so I nipped down the hall, opened the door and I couldn't believe my eyes. There he was grumbling menacingly. Back to the kitchen I went and there he was again on the doorstep. I was beginning to think there were two of them. I was never more pleased to see anybody than the family coming home and when they did, that dog's nature changed completely to one of friendship, wagging his tail and even licking my hand as I went on my way."*

Father always like to have a well trained sheepdog and one that he could be proud of to see working well. He often said a good dog is as good as another man. A number of the dogs we owned were trained by a friend of his called Amos. He had a hill farm in Wensleydale where he used to work and train dogs as another means of income. The first time I went with father to see about a new dog, I was completely mesmerised by his whistle. He was working two dogs amongst the heather and across a wide valley where they were hardly visible, and to me looked about two miles away. Putting his fingers to his lips, a single blast was enough to control either dog, making them do exactly as he wanted. The whistle was ear-splitting standing by his side and I dearly wished to be able to copy the sound. I asked him to show me the secret, and after two or three abortive attempts, when all I could muster was the sound of rushing air, he finally said, *"Nay lad, thee mouths wrong shape."* After much practice, weeks later, I did manage to produce a sound that passed as a whistle using two fingers, but one that any self-respecting dog would ignore completely.

Amos was a man of few words and his wife spoke even less, and in all my visits, I don't ever remember seeing her in clothes other than a bonnet and skirts down to the ground. All I ever heard her say were *'Ester dun'* and *'ketels on'*, but her cup of tea, scones and homemade butter was unbeatable. After his initial greeting, Amos too lapsed into virtual silence. An odd grunt, *'ugh ugh' 'aye'* and *'nay lad'* seemed to be the extent of his vocabulary, but then dad could *'talk the hind leg off a donkey'*, as the saying goes, and probably didn't give him a chance to say much. However, his dogs understood every sign and whistle he made and his knowledge of training dogs left a deep impression on me.

Rover was trained by Amos, and a rather unlikely looking sheepdog he was. He had been bred on our farm, being a son of Roy. Rover had long shaggy hair and was a uniform sandy colour, having what could only be described as a goatee beard. He had gone up to the moors when one year old to learn his trade. Amos once said, in one of his more talkative moods, that *"they were not strong enough to work the moor until they had reached that age and so long as they knew right from wrong, did as they were told and had a brain in their head, that was all that was required from a dog and he would teach them everything else they needed to know."* He maintained his dogs were in need of a rest after around two years of the heavy moor land work, and it was at this age when he let them go to the lowland farms where life was a little easier for them. Rover, however, was such a favourite and good at this job, Amos asked if he could keep him another year or two and in fact, it was almost six years before Rover returned to us, just before the war started in 1939. As we collected him, Amos gave another long speech saying, *"He is the best dog I have ever owned or likely to, make sure he enjoys the rest of his life, he's earned that already."*

When we got him back, he had lost some of his speed but none of his prowess. He was a master of his craft where sheep were concerned and moved cattle with apparent ease. I think both sensed he had a certain authority that should on no account be disregarded. He used to save miles of walking, through his ability to round up stock on the farm, and if sheep were to be taken to the local market, you could safely ride in the car in front and rely on him to follow up behind, never allowing them to stray. My goats, however, had him completely baffled, as they had not been taught to respect the authority of a dog, while to Rover they looked like sheep, but certainly didn't behave like them. The two kids used to tease, even to dancing on his kennel roof, and Squeak just put her head down and charged, which when you have been taught not to retaliate, was hardly playing the game. They finally came to a compromise, Rover taking a wide berth when the goats were around and the goats doing just the same as they did before he arrived on the scene.

Rover will also be remembered for his bladder capacity, which seemed to be the most copious of all the dogs I have known. If a car came on to the yard you could be certain it would be christened, but he would not be satisfied with wetting one wheel, it would be all four, and the spare if he could reach it. An authenticated record of all four wheels on each of three cars was once accomplished '*in one continual motion*', if you will excuse the pun. He too soon realised that the army cooks were there to be exploited and if he was missing when his services were required, the cook-house was the first place to look and that is where he would invariably be found.

Next came Blue. During one of the school holidays I went over to the little market town of Thirsk, where each Monday there was an auction of poultry and other bits and pieces, which was held behind the Three Tuns Hotel, just off the town square. This was a favourite place of mine to visit, as besides the poultry of various kinds, there used to be a number of pet animals up for sale. One time I was there, I heard a farmer tell his son to go out into the market place for half a dozen eggs, and on his return they were put into a cage containing a few scraggy hens to give the impression they were laying, and therefore bring a few pence more. (Tricks of the trade).

It was at this auction I bought Blue. He cost me twenty pence, and the name seemed appropriate to me as he was a blue roan in colour and he also had one blue eye (the other was brown), a peculiarity known as a wall eye and not uncommon in dogs. However, in Blue it had the effect of giving him a most comical appearance especially when he stood with one ear cocked and the other drooping. I think it was this look that appealed to me because I had no intention of buying a dog when I went there. His parentage was doubtful, but obviously mainly sheepdog and somewhere along the line there was probably a touch of whippet, because he was so quick, I am certain he could have won at the White City Stadium. He was a dog that loved company, was quick to learn and forever trying to please. He soon learnt all the basic rules and before letting him loose on father's sheep, I trained him to round up our ducks, which together with the other poultry were in mother's hands, and I felt I could manipulate her better if anything went wrong.

He showed such promise rounding up the ducks and geese that father suggested letting Amos have him to finish his training. This duly happened and we got, or to be more precise father, got Sam in return, as by this time Rover was being pensioned off and now spent most of his time in the camp kitchen, where he found rich pickings. Rover frequently accompanied the soldiers on their visits to the local hostelries, and they too noticed his watering talents, one claiming he cocked his leg forty two times on the journey back to camp, probably in competition with the troops, not unknown for their aptitude to the local brew.

Some time later I heard that Amos was quite pleased with Blue, but not as a sheepdog. In his opinion he was convinced he would never make a sheepdog, but worth his weight in gold for catching rabbits.

Sam was a powerfully built smooth coated black and white collie and equally good with cattle and sheep, ideal for the mixed collection of stock on the farm, but as time went on he was found to have a number of vices. One asset was his ability to dispose of rats which he did with great alacrity and many evenings were spent with Bob, one of the farm hands, together with his dog and Sam, after rats around the farm and adjoining hedgerows. At the time, I was a little intrigued as to why the tails were cut off the rats and carefully stored in a small bag. Bob's excuse was so he could keep account of the numbers caught. I found out later that the tails went to the local authority for which there was a bounty of one penny per tail which over the year paid for his dog licence, and helped to keep him in beer money.

Sam hated dark uniforms. Whether he had had an unfortunate experience concerning one I don't know, but policemen and postmen seemed to be especially at risk, and we always tried to keep him out of the way when they were about. Another of his failings was his love for eggs; he would eat them one after another given the chance. I suppose he got the taste from Amos whose basic diet for all his dogs was a mixture of milk, eggs and flaked maize, ingredients that could be found on most stock farms at that time. Fortunately for us, the deep litter method of keeping poultry was coming in then and we only had a few hens scratching about on free range. Consequently there were few eggs around for him to pick up, but he knew all the likely nesting sites and would regularly do his rounds in the hope of finding a quick snack.

Sam's worse vice by far, and probably caused by the latter one, was one of flatulence. Outside it was of no consequence but if he was sitting in the kitchen at the time, the situation could be so nauseating, that poor old Sam was seldom allowed the comfort of an open fire. Although extremely good at his job on the farm and for company, Sam could never be fully trusted with other dogs; he probably had a small streak of jealousy in his makeup and never really took to old Rover as a companion. I think the feeling however, may have been mutual, as Rover wasn't too keen on Sam. Everybody missed Rover when he passed away and I would like to think he enjoyed his leisurely retirement, following the years of hard work running round the moors in his youth.

Because of Sam's dislike of his own sex, Peggy was brought in to replace Rover. She was a small, golden coloured bitch with a beautiful nature, and another who was always trying to please. She had a habit of curling her lips up which gave the impression that she was trying to smile, and I was certain that is what she intended it to be, and this smile would usually be accompanied with a sidling movement as she tried to wrap herself round your legs. Sam seemed to appreciate the attempt to find him acceptable company and it also made him more perverse in his attitude to other dogs, looking upon Peggy as his personal property. She seemed to resent his overbearing intentions, and preferred human company much to his disgust.

Peggy was memorable for both stamina and speed; she loved riding in the car, hated to be left at home and given the opportunity would follow the car if we left without her. Once we drove to Boroughbridge Auction Market and had just parked the car and were walking through the gate when she came in to meet us. I reckoned she was about twenty times faster over the distance than it took my cousin and me to walk the donkeys home from there. She also had the ability to recognise our car, as on another occasion she was racing down the road as we were heading back home. As the car approached she immediately stopped, whether by sight or smell I don't know, but as we passed, she turned and started to follow us back, and taking pity on her, the car was halted and she got her ride home.

Cats and dogs do not generally mix, but it would be inappropriate to pass this stage without a mention of Thomas.

He was a tomcat, but in many ways as much like a dog as a cat. Cats were a feature on most farms and we always had a small contingent, supplemented from time to time with the wandering minstrels, as father used to call the stray cats that frequently turned up, his favourites being a strain of tortoiseshell cats that seemed to have been with us forever. At milking times, morning and night, they would turn up from all directions for the warm milk, put down for them to drink in reward for their efforts to keep the rodent population down to acceptable numbers. Thomas arrived at one such feeding time, from where he came was never determined. He stood out from the rest of the cats being almost twice as big as the largest of them, and he was strikingly handsome, his colour best described as a blue tabby. He was, however, extremely wary of people and I tried to gain his confidence by talking to him. It was obvious he was hungry and wanted some of the fresh milk, but wouldn't allow me to get within yards of him, bolting whenever I approached. He stayed around and gradually over the next few weeks began to accept titbits when thrown towards him, where previously I think he thought they were thrown at him, and finally condescended to let me stroke him. It was another week or so before he let me pick him up and it was then I realised he wasn't carrying as much flesh as he should have had, and had probably been short of food since leaving his former home.

As mother did not dislike cats, though did not encourage the farm cats to come into the house, I thought Thomas would make a nice house pet and accordingly made the introduction. Following her generous feeding, combined with a worming pill scrounged from our vet, and which probably went on father's account, he rapidly put on weight and in his prime weighed a little over fourteen pounds. He wasn't officially allowed to stay indoors at night, and some people expecting him to earn his keep catching vermin, but I suspect this was something he had never had to do and certainly wasn't about to start if he could avoid it. He soon worked out, he could climb onto a handily placed outhouse, up onto the roof and through my bedroom window, purposefully left open to allow his entry, and then spend a comfortable night on the foot of my bed. Despite denials that this was occurring, the evidence was rather damning in wet weather, with the dirty footprints all over the bedspread. Thomas had quite a reserved nature and was never really happy with strangers, quick to disappear from view should visitors call, but in our company had the loudest purr of any cat I have heard, which is rather unusual for male cats, not normally renowned for purring.

Thomas was a great wanderer, and during his life with me, was seen in at least three local villages, no doubt doing what tom cats do best, although I must admit, I never saw any kittens either on the farm or elsewhere, resembling him. As he often came home with battle scars, he was obviously mixing it with his rivals for the attention of the female cat population in our area.

Thomas was the first cat that made me realise how individual they are, each having their own personality and since he came into my life I have admired their sense of freedom and above all their independent attitude which they so obviously expect you to accept. This is rather unlike the majority of dogs who are quite happy for you to be the master.

Chapter 3

At Home on the Farm

Another ambition had been realised, that of leaving school. I loved the free and easy country life and was never one for being organised and having to follow a routine existence, and couldn't have been happier when the time came to say goodbye to lessons. Though ever since grateful for my grammar school education, at school I could see no reason whatsoever why Latin, a dead and forgotten language as far as I was concerned, should be included in the curriculum, Later I wished I had taken a little more notice, when I became involved in the zoological world, where everything has a Latin name recognised worldwide, though it was somewhat surprising how words long forgotten came back easily. Perhaps the school authorities are a little cleverer than school children give them credit for.

When I left school, I had no thoughts other than working at home and following an agricultural career in the family tradition, and so the day after leaving, found me continuing to do just what I had been doing during the holidays and in my spare time.

At that time a herd of pedigree Friesian cattle was being developed on the farm to replace the shorthorn breeds which were going out of fashion, in the hope that a higher milk yield would be produced for the same amount of effort. On the arable side, although tractors were beginning to be more and more popular, we still relied on horsepower of the four-legged kind. If it is agreed that dogs are man's best friend, I think anybody with a practical knowledge of horses, would agree with me that they surely come a close second.

Some of the horses on the farm at Sharow, 1944.

Horse dealing seemed to be a recognised pastime in the farming fraternity, and the pursuit of this practise was probably also used as an excuse to get out and about and visit other farms to exchange gossip. Ever since I can remember, there was a procession of horses to and from the farm. Generally though, there was a core of proven working horses that could be trusted to do the work in hand, and stayed on the farm while others came and went, hopefully putting a few pounds profit into the business.

One horse that came during the war was a heavy hunter with a famous name, April the Fifth, probably named after the famous racehorse, and coincidently sharing his name with my birthday. I think father had ideas of using him in the milk float we had for delivering milk at the time, but never got around to doing it, although he did use him with saddle and bridle to visit outlying fields when checking the stock.

Whereas father was quite a proficient rider, my experience was confined to riding lumbering carthorses back from the fields, a gentle pony, and the donkeys. Nevertheless, I had ideas of emulating famous jockeys one day with April, and saddled him up, and using a mounting block in the yard, scaled the height needed to get on his back. The walk to the nearest field was uneventful, the next hundred yards wasn't, as in seconds he reached the first fence, which I hadn't even considered jumping, but he obviously had. To his credit he did come back to look for me, but I had already decided that the Grand National wasn't my scene, and he went back to the stable. I also remember April for two other reasons, firstly because the big chestnut used to get really excited at the sound of the bugle on the army camp. I assume it was because he associated it with his hunting days, and he would gallop madly round the fields taking hedges in his stride. Secondly, for the extremely tight jodhpurs covering the ample seat of his previous lady owner, who, after selling him to father, occasionally visited the farm to renew the relationship and take April for a gallop round the fields. I was convinced that the trousers would split as they bounced up and down on the saddle, but if they did, I wasn't around to see it happen.

For years we had provided a milk round, the milk being delivered twice a day round the villages, but this was fortunately cut to one delivery during the war years. Kitty was a dales pony who had pulled the milk float, doing this chore for more years than I can remember and had come with us from our previous farm, and doubled as a riding pony for my sister and me. However, unlike April, her normal gait was at best a comfortable trot otherwise an amiable walk, and she was unlikely to unseat the least untrained rider. Kitty knew the milk round by heart, together with every stop and would take the float unattended, always being in the right place at the right time knowing also where she could expect a titbit from one of the customers, and would wait there anticipating the treat. Kitty was put out to grass, as the saying goes, when a smart new van was acquired for the deliveries, and finally passed away at the age of twenty-eight.

It is worth mentioning that the vehicle that replaced her didn't save any time whatsoever, the round taking just as long as it did with the pony. It didn't get half the attention, it had none of the character, probably cost twice as much to run, and it's called progress.

Over the ensuing years names like Major, Captain, Blossom, Beaut and Price stick in the mind, and the impression left of these powerful shire horses working together on the land, to me gives a far truer portrayal of an English rural scene than the present day tractors rushing about.

Six o'clock was, then, the accepted time to start work in the morning, and arguably of all the farm work, walking into a stable at that time was the least traumatic, especially when there was a frost in the air. On opening the stable door, you would be met with a welcoming whinny from one or more of the horses and then the heat from their bodies would hit you. That together with the scent of hay, leather and the horses themselves would be most agreeable, although no doubt there would be some who would disagree. It was on these cold winter mornings you would find it took a little longer to finish the cleaning and grooming, and of course on wet days you could spend hours in the adjoining harness room cleaning the leather and polishing the brasses, so that the horses would look their best when taken out to work.

The old saying that *'a willing horse gets the most work'*, is certainly true, as, if I was given a one horse task then Captain, a seventeen and a half hand grey shire would usually be my choice. He must have weighed close to a tonne and could easily pull his own weight, a true gentle giant in the horse world. He once stood on my foot causing me to lose my big toe nail and I still have a crooked toe to prove it.

Stallions were not kept on the farm and it used to be quite an event when one of these huge animals visited to perform their natural function. When they appeared, young children were usually told to clear off and play somewhere, but in the event, little faces would be seen round any convenient corner hoping to see everything in detail.

It was following one of these visits, eleven months later to be precise, that Grace's foal was born. She was another grey shire and usually partnered Captain in tandem together, an almost identical pair in looks if not in sex. Disastrously, Grace did not survive due to complications in the birth, but her foal did.

It was not unusual to have young animals of one sort or another being reared artificially, so another did not seem too much of a challenge. Father said he had once reared a foal on cow's milk many years ago and it had been called Charlie, so Grace's foal was christened Charlie, which seemed to please him, and I was designated to look after the new arrival.

Charlie seemed to be all head and legs, and he was almost completely black, as I remember was his father, with four white socks and a white star on his forehead. He was standing on his long legs within half an hour of his birth and ready for his first feed. Being used to feeding pet lambs with a bottle, I thought it would be a simple matter to give a foal a bottle of milk, but how wrong can you be. This was a process he hadn't been born to accept and wouldn't if he could get away with it, showing spirit from the start. He decided that it should be a nice soft teat oozing warm mothers milk, not a lump of rubber stuck on a bottle of cows' milk. The first feed was finally accomplished, with him lying on the straw and me in a similar position, and more milk on the floor than down his throat. Each ensuing feed however, became gradually easier, until a few weeks later I would be almost knocked down in the rush to get at it. Being born in the spring meant he was soon able to go out and quickly learn how to eat grass, and experiment with anything else that looked remotely edible. As he was raised artificially, I suppose it was inevitable that he would prefer human company to that of other animals, and did not like to be left with them without my presence. Mother used to call him *'Mary's little lamb'* because everywhere I went he was sure to go, although, at the time I wasn't too happy with the analogy, and would probably have preferred Batman and Robin. He grew at an incredible rate, admittedly a little preferential treatment helped, but he was much larger than another foal of similar age and reared by its mother, and also showed far more intelligence.

Charlie did not need any breaking in, as he was used to a halter from day one and other pieces of harness as the weeks went by. The first time he was put in a cart, I expected fireworks, but it was accepted without flinching. The only time he objected to anything, was the first time he visited the blacksmith to have his first set of shoes fitted.

I had taught him a few tricks in his first year which were later regretted as he was quite adept at opening doors and gates, and if put out in a pasture, it wasn't long before he was trotting back into the yard, so we were constantly devising other methods of securing the field gates.

Unfortunately sentiment cannot be taken into account when farming, the animals being rather like goods in a shop, and when Charlie was three years old, he was one of the three horses sold to raise the capital required to buy our first tractor, to keep pace with the rapidly developing farming methods. Although it was a wrench to see him go at the time, I did see him again some years later, competing in a ploughing match. Although I doubt very much whether he recognised me, it was obvious that he had found a very good home, and it did give some pleasure to see him looking so fit, and upholding the traditions of a true working horse.

Chapter 4

One Became Two Plus Three

Wiseacres tell us that schooldays are the happiest days of your life although it didn't work that way for me. Granted there were happy days whilst I was at school, but the best times came later. After the war ended, life was lived to the full; I became quite involved with sport, playing cricket and football never really succumbing to the finer arts of rugby, we were supposed to enjoy at school. Fortunately father was keen on sports, having been a reasonable cricketer in his younger days, and he fully supported my endeavours in this field.

I had reached the grand age of twenty-five when I took the plunge and married, deciding it was almost time to settle down. My wife, Maveen, was a local girl, and both our parents had known each other since their childhood days, both fathers actually having gone to school together. A cottage on the farm was redecorated, altered to our immediate requirements, and looking extremely habitable, when out of the blue an opportunity for a post of farms manager on a large agricultural enterprise near York was offered, through a contact in the Young Farmers Club, of which I had been a member for a number of years.

Father suggested it would be an excellent chance for further experience and could lead to a more financially rewarding future, as our farm was thought hardly capable of supporting both families. I think he had quickly worked out that I would not be using his car so much either, and that he would save a fortune in petrol charges on his account if I went.

I accepted the post, and on our return from honeymoon, instead of moving into our farm cottage, we found ourselves moving into a charming old world cottage situated in the middle of a picture postcard village.

Anybody not experienced in village life as it was then, would find it hard to visualise just how friendly country folk could be, everybody knew each other and had time for a chat and to pass the time of day. We never wanted for fresh vegetables; these would appear on the doorstep, left by enthusiastic gardeners and without any thought of reward. Any of the neighbours going to town, the nearest being about five miles distant, would enquire if we needed any shopping, or bring back any outstanding orders. We for our part tried to do the same for them.

We had a friendly gamekeeper who would make sure the heating was on if we were away, have the house warm for our return, and look after the garden in our absence. He would also provide a brace of rabbits, on request, for a change in our diet. I used to enjoy a young roast rabbit for dinner prior to myxomatosis appearing, having been introduced, and reaching the estate in 1955. It was a most horrible disease causing a high mortality in the rabbit population, and completely put me off eating them ever since. Unfortunately the disease is still with us today.

We both considered ourselves fortunate in having such a tranquil existence, in the peaceful surroundings of East Yorkshire, for the first years of our life together.

Luckily, or maybe it was foreordained, my wife shared

my love of animals, with perhaps one exception, in her uneasiness where bats are concerned (those of the non-cricketing variety). This fear was well illustrated shortly after moving into our old cottage. Early one morning, far too early to be awake, she disturbed me from my slumbers saying there was something in the bedroom. Turning the light on it became patently obvious that there were, three pipistrelle bats doing aerobatics round the bedroom, and from that moment on, she took no further part in the proceedings, as she was underneath the bedclothes. It was probably as well she didn't observe the following few minutes, a naked body trying to direct three whirling bats through an open window may have been just too much to bear. I didn't seem to be having too much success with my efforts to remove the bats, and then suddenly thought; *"What if the neighbours are watching. I've got the light on and the curtains are open, they will be wondering what sort of deviation their new neighbours are up to in the middle of the night."* Hastily I picked up a torch and switched off the electric light, as a muffled voice from under the clothes said, *"Have they gone?"* and before I could answer no, they had, one after another gone out through the window, and into the night, obviously seeing better in the dark than they could in artificial lighting. It was quite some time before I was allowed to sleep with the window open after that episode.

It wasn't long before we found something else to look after. On the Yorkshire Wolds, there is a very popular smaller breed of dog which elsewhere would probably be called a Jack Russell terrier, but on the Wolds it is known as an Earth Terrier. Originally bred for bolting foxes they became popular because of their outstanding ability to kill rats. On one particular farm I visited, they had a particularly attractive strain, most of which were white with tan markings about the head, and as there was litter of puppies there at the time, naturally I acquired one.

Snip, we christened him, was just seven weeks old and small enough to sit inside a pint pot, and when fully grown was no more than a foot long and about seven inches high. What was lacking in stature was more than made up in spirit, as he was a dog that was fun to own, full of life and always ready for a game.

All four of our parents suggested at the time he would be more trouble than a baby, I think secretly wishing he had been, and looking forward to their first grandchild. Father however, was more than impressed when Snip killed three rats in as many seconds, when they shot out nose to tail from a drainpipe on his farm, on one of our visits there.

Maxine and Snip, 1958.

Our parents got their wish for a grandchild when our daughter, Maxine, was born a year later and Snip howled in unison to her cries, a sound completely new from him and which took us by surprise, reminiscent of old Roy all those years ago. There was some little doubt in our minds whether Snip would be jealous of our new arrival, after being the centre of attraction for so long, but this was not the case at all. Although he could be a little hooligan at times, he was ever so gentle with Maxine, and she in turn came to adore his attentions.

Like many Yorkshire men, cricket was a second religion, and I still had a passion for playing the game which had developed from my schooldays. I joined a local club, and the weekend games were more like social occasions for the players families, even it the game itself was very keenly contested. Each weekend, therefore, our small estate car was packed with wife, baby, dog, pram, food and cricket gear to travel to wherever we happened to be playing, Most of the matches were annual affairs between the teams, and the families of both sides would join forces to chaperone both children and dogs and supervise the interval between innings, when picnics and food were had by all.

Our second child, Philip, was almost born at one such match, when following a false alarm on the Friday evening, I was persuaded to turn out for the usual Saturday game. We set out as normal with the full regalia, plus another bag ready packed in case it should be needed. The ground we were playing at that particular weekend was situated in a large private park, which was reached by travelling about a mile down a rather bumpy drive. I had already warned Maveen that if I was nearing a century in a run chase it would be no use shouting if the worst should happen, and quickly arrange alternative transport to the nursing home. Fortunately, it didn't, and we got through the match without incident, but I am convinced the bumpy ride down that drive contributed to Philip's arrival the next day.

We were at one such Saturday match, when somebody

mentioned that strange sounds were emanating from our car. Fearing the worst, I went over to where it was parked, and was a little surprised to see it rocking slightly, the movement accompanied by peculiar snuffles and grunts. It turned out to be a friend's pet bulldog, who, looking for a bit of shade away from the hot sun, had wedged himself firmly beneath the vehicle, and then being firmly stuck, was unable to extricate himself. A few willing hands quickly lifted the car with the help of the jack, and removed the offending animal, none the worse for its adventure.

A local rugby club ran a popular knock-out cricket competition for teams in the area, and the village side, having a successful run one year, got through to the final and went on to win the cup. That of course entailed staying at the ground longer, in the club bar to celebrate the victory, and a good time was had by all, including little Snip, who by the end of the evening had much difficulty in walking a straight line. He had always liked a drop of liquid refreshment, and on this occasion had been given far too many sips from far too many glasses and was quite inebriated. The following day, it did not seem to affect him the following day as much as some of the cricketers who had accompanied him the night before, nor did he show any ill effects afterwards, and it certainly didn't stop him from enjoying his little tipples later, whenever the opportunity arose.

After five years in the East Riding of Yorkshire, I was asked by my employer if I would like to go to Lancashire to supervise his agricultural holdings in that county, and as it entailed a more *"hands on"* approach, I accepted. I had always preferred to be doing things rather than overseeing others, so a more active life on the farms, doing a more manual job, appealed.

It was with a little regret that we left our cricketing

friends who had organised a going away party for us, and our young family, plus Snip, moved from our comfortable cottage, into a five bed-roomed farmhouse not far from Blackpool. On a clear day it was possible to see the lift going up the tower from our windows, and on our arrival our herdsman told me the tower itself could be used as a good weather guide, saying that if you could see it clearly it would probably rain, and if you couldn't see it, it was raining. We found the weather in Lancashire was not quite as bad as it was painted.

Soon it was time for our children to start collecting pets, just as I had done at their age. I remember Maxine's first hamster disappearing into the settee and remaining at liberty in the rambling farmhouse for about two weeks before being captured in one of the bedrooms. However, how it managed to find food and drink during its freedom will remain a mystery, but it had certainly done very well for itself, and was looking quite plump. The biggest question mark over the event, was how it had managed to evade Snip, who would not have allowed the hamster to roam over his territory unless they had formed some sort of alliance. Once the children started going to school, more exotic pets were envisaged, and it wasn't long before such things as stick insects and moon moth caterpillars were adorning the sideboard and other surfaces, things no doubt I would have had in my youth, had they been available. A large pet shop in Preston became their favourite hunting ground and whenever time allowed, I used to get badgered in to taking them there to see if anything new had been acquired. One Saturday they spotted a fairly large monitor lizard, and thought that it would make an unusual pet. The lizard was duly purchased and questions about its diet and housing answered. On the way home, of course, they had had to look inside the box to see if it was still alright, and the monitor immediately saw its chance of freedom, and disappeared under the front seat of the car. He had to stay there until we arrived home, where the driver's seat had to be partly dismantled to get the animal out.

Buster, as he was called, was installed in a large glass-fronted cage complete with heater and bath, and he actually proved to be quite intelligent and did not appear to dislike being handled. It soon became evident, and probably inevitable, that Buster wasn't going to be confined to his cage, and was soon to be seen running around the living room. He discovered a hiding place in a narrow space between the sideboard and the wall, and used to wedge himself in there. He would happily stay there for hours till the spirit moved him, and then he would drop with a loud plop onto the floor and scoot across the carpet beneath the settee, or to another suitable spot, and as by now he was almost a yard long, he would terrify unprepared visitors. After living with Buster for about two years he was really getting too big to manage correctly. The proprietor of the pet shop agreed to exchange him for an Amazon parrot, which seemed to me an excellent deal as I had always had an ambition to own a parrot and thought if we kept Buster much longer, we had a good chance of losing a few friends.

The parrot was a young bird, and we named him Rocky. Rocky, too, spent more time out of the cage than in it; the only time he went in was to feed. His favourite perch when he became efficient at flying, was on the top of the fluorescent light in the kitchen from where he could watch all the comings and goings. He had a habit of dropping straight down from this perch and into the sink to do his ablutions, subsequently splashing and shaking, and putting water everywhere, before going back to his perch to preen. Rocky had clearly been held captive for some time in one of the South American villages, as he would mutter away for ages in an alien tongue, obviously imitating his captor, and cackle like hens that had probably been close to his cage. I often thought it would be interesting to get an interpreter so I could know what the incessant chatter was about, but the way he ranted at times led me to think that it may be a little embarrassing. He was a talented mimic and would copy Snip barking, just like the real thing, and the dog would think there was an intruder in the house. Rocky could also imitate the children's voices so well that when he called mum or dad, you would find yourself foolishly answering him, thinking it was them calling.

We were soon to lose little Snip in a traffic accident, and the house felt so empty without him. Ever since we first had him, he used to enjoy a little game we had of *"hunt the slipper"*, the original one I gave him to cut his teeth on. We used to hide his slipper in all sorts of places and tell him to find it, which he always did unerringly, but he turned the tables on us, as he used to hide ours, and there was never a pair of slippers to be found together in the house. Snip, running about with a slipper, was the thing I missed most when he had gone. It's was extraordinary how you get used to having dogs around, taking their presence for granted, only to miss them so greatly when they go.

One Sunday afternoon, some time later, we were out for a ride in the car when the children spotted a sign on the roadside proclaiming, *"Puppies for Sale, Enquire Within."* I probably didn't require a lot of persuading to stop and enquire, but should have known better, because half an hour later we owned a boxer pup.

As he grew, Bruno became the most exasperating animal I have ever owned, as whilst being completely trustworthy with the children and one of the best playmates you could wish to have for them, it was impossible to keep him at home. I am certain he could scent a bitch on heat a mile away, and once he got that scent he was off. I think we should have named him Casanova as it would certainly have been more appropriate. His most usual venue was a smallholding adjoining the farm where the owners had similar interests to our own as far as animals were concerned. Here you would find about a dozen dogs of varying ancestry, together with cattle, goats, cats, ducks etc., in such numbers that it was always advisable to watch where you were putting your feet. As the smallholding could be reached without going onto a road, it was quite safe to let the children go to collect Bruno whenever his nose had taken him in that direction. One day on such a visit to collect Bruno, Philip came home with a large, evil-smelling billy goat, as well as the dog, saying *"Mr Thompson has given him to me."* I had a good idea then how my father must have felt when I arrived home with some of my acquisitions. But to give credit to both children, they went to work with a will on Billy, shampooing him and polishing his horns, which were about three feet wide, until he was almost unrecognisable and looked more like a show animal than the disreputable creature that arrived, and he even smelt sweeter. The goat seemed to look forward to all the attention they gave him and would walk around on a lead as good as any dog. He also saved me the job of cutting the grass so often in the orchard, where he looked quite presentable, and was admired by a number of visitors.

Being in a rural area where farming was the main occupation, I thought it advisable to let Bruno go, due to the concentration of stock, especially sheep, in the district. I would not have been at all pleased should he have disturbed any farm animals on his amorous visits, even though I was reasonably confident that it would not have been done with evil intent. As it happened, some of our friends from Ireland were looking for a mature dog at the time, and taking a shine to the boisterous nature of Bruno, were only too pleased to take him off our hands, even after being told of his depravity. They told us later how well he had settled in and become such an excellent companion, and also how he had greatly embarrassed them on one occasion when they were talking to their local priest, who was holding his Labrador bitch at the time. All I could say was, *"Well, you were warned."*

It was about this time when father decided to retire from farming, and his farm was sold. It was a decision requiring some thought, but I was quite happy in the work I was doing and did not wish to persuade him to keep the venture going. I did, however, inherit Fly from him. Fly was a black and white Border collie bitch he was working at the time and he thought she should be useful with our stock, rather than letting her go to somebody strange. We already had Prince, another border collie, on the farm, and as working dogs they formed a formidable pair. Prince was a strong dog, suited for driving cattle and Fly proved to be most intelligent living up to the build up she had been given by father. I once took her up into the fields during the lambing season, and noticing a ewe was in difficulty, told her to sit whilst I went over to the sheep to give the assistance needed with the birth. I then went on my way, completely forgetting Fly who was patiently waiting. Later in the day I missed her, wanting to go on another trip round the ewes, and when I looked she was in exactly the same place as I had left her in the morning, waiting for her next order.

With the two dogs living together, it was only natural to expect we would have an increase in dog numbers and before long the inevitable happened, and Fly had a litter of puppies, most of which were reserved before they were born. We kept one bitch puppy to train as a replacement, who turned out to be Lassie, and looked upon as a family pet, spending as much time in the house as outside.

The children spoilt Lassie, who was brushed and combed more than any show dog, her nails were manicured and even her teeth cleaned, a practice she seemed to enjoy, I assume, from the minty taste of the toothpaste which had a habit of disappearing from the bathroom.

I think I may have to share the blame for her taste in mint, because Lassie had an addiction to polo mints which she usually shared with me. I had got into the habit of carrying a packet to ease the craving for tobacco which I had recently given up, following one of the Chancellor's annual hypes, and found Lassie would practically ask for one whenever I took them from my pocket. She was about a year old when our third child, Simon, was born and she would sit for hours at the side of the pram and follow wherever he was taken. I have noticed time and time again how a dog seems to sense that a young child is helpless and requires looking after, and some sort of affinity is bonded between the two. Collies seem particularly inclined to take on this responsibility without any persuasion whatsoever.

Lassie had the typical collie temperament, loyal and protective towards the family, but reserved with other people almost to the point of totally ignoring them completely, but I would not have trusted her not to have attacked any stranger coming between her and the children who adored her. Having a dog of this nature when you are residing in an isolated position is without doubt one of the best deterrents possible, as with Lassie in the house we could be sure nobody would get as far as the back door before she would let us know they were there.

**Maxine with Lassie and pup at
Weeton near Blackpool, 1964.**

We were fortunate to have on the farm a pair of resident barn owls who had made their home in one of the buildings. Each year they would rear their young in a nest box strategically placed, so we could watch their progress, and development of the chicks from an adjacent window, and it was almost beyond belief the number of mice and voles they would bring in to feed their offspring, even hunting in daylight over the fields at times. They were rearing chicks halfway through our eighth year at the farm when the adult pair disappeared, never to be seen again, where or how they went we never knew, but as they were such wonderful parents, we were certain it was not of their own doing. Subsequently, we found their three young owlets on the ground in different corners of the barn, in various stages of development, the largest having feathers and within days of being able to fly, the smallest still showing downy fluff through newly growing feathers. Having had some experience many years ago with Ollie the tawny owl, I set the family the task of finding food, which proved to be far more difficult than I had anticipated. Certainly the mouse population on the farm decreased somewhat, but it made us realise how much cleverer the owls were at catching them than we are, so we descended on our favourite pet shop who was good enough to give us some of his unsold stock, only to find that they were not sufficient for the ever open mouths. That was when we found strips of chicken were equally acceptable for their enormous appetites, the chicken first being rolled in small feathers to aid the owl's digestion and help form the regurgitated pellet.

All three owls were successfully reared and eventually released into their parent's old habitat, and two of them were still resident there when we moved on a couple of years later. The third owl disappeared a few weeks after release and although never seeing it again, we often wondered what became of it, hoping it had found a sanctuary in a neighbouring barn and a mate to settle with.

It was spring and the farm a hive of industry and work on the arable fields well under way. The birds had started to build nests in the surrounding hedgerows and the hedgehogs and other small mammals were becoming active. It seemed to me, as I went about my business, rather sad that modern farming methods are not very conducive to the preservation of our nature. I recalled the time when horsemen working the land would find time to move a plovers nest and eggs three or four times during cultivation of a field, to give the bird a chance to hatch and rear their young. Today's heavy tractors and large implements, working at four times the speed, means there is little time for such activities, even if they were seen. Hares too are vulnerable to land cultivations, the leverets being born into a shallow scrape or depression in a field and their natural colouring making them almost invisible, blending in with the colour of the earth. As they are born coinciding with the preparation for sowing spring corn, many must perish as the tractors and implements speed over the ground.

Harold was born in a ploughed field due to be sown with barley. I found him a few yards from his dead sibling, both presumably having passed beneath a set of harrows working the field. After some consideration I thought the best chance the leveret would have for survival would be to take him home and attempt to rear him. If left he would certainly not survive further field work and if moved to a safe position in the hedgerow, would be more likely to be found by a predator than his mother.

Maxine took on the responsibility of feeding Harold, starting with diluted cows' milk, gradually increasing it to full strength; he was initially fed drop by drop from an eye dropper but soon becoming efficient at emptying it quickly. His early home was a large cardboard box, but as he grew he was given far more freedom. He was great fun to be with, not many people can boast of living with a hare about the house, some probably would not want to, but those that haven't, missed an unforgettable experience.

Once on solid food, we found sufficient for him in the house without having to purchase any special diet, porridge oats, cornflakes, biscuits, most vegetables and apples were readily taken. Sweet biscuits were a favourite food and a box of these was usually kept in a cupboard in the living room. One leap would take him to the top of a nearby armchair and a knowing look at the cupboard was enough to tell us what he wanted. Most journeys around the house were completed at full gallop and loose mats on polished floors ending up anywhere but where they should be. Lassie was fully aware that Harold was one of the family and would tolerate being pestered by him, until he got into a really playful mood, and then she would go to the door, making it known that she wanted to go out for a bit of peace.

Harold loved the sun and would follow the rays coming through the windows, stretching out to get the full benefit, and if the opportunity arose we would find him in one of the southerly facing bedrooms laid on top of a bed in a most unhare like pose. He was devoted to Maxine and she doted on him, and when she wasn't at school they were always together, either inside or out. Outside the house he was just the same, tearing around at full gallop and living life to the full. We had to be a little careful where the working dogs were concerned, but the farm cats were absolutely terrified of him, as he would stand high on his hind legs and a threat from his waving front legs would send them scuttling for cover. Having felt the power of those front feet on a few occasions myself, and then when he was supposed to be playing, I didn't blame them in the least.

At two years old, Harold was three feet long when laid out in his favourite position, and very powerful with it, but he still had a liking for biscuits and a drink of milk and was as friendly as ever. He had ample opportunities to go off into the fields but seemingly having got accustomed to the comforts of home, preferred that to the wide open spaces. He was well into his third year when Maxine was given the chance to go on an extended holiday, which was taken even though there were reservations about having to leave her beloved Harold behind.

As it turned out, her worst fears were justified, because he missed her company greatly and despite all our efforts to entice him, after a couple of weeks practically refused to eat anything. Even veterinary advice was insufficient to save him and eventually he became so weak and undernourished he died just two days before Maxine came home. His passing was greatly mourned by all the family and I think even the cats missed him. His grave, out in the orchard next to little Snip, was planted with daffodil bulbs and carefully tended thereafter. I often wondered what Snip would have made of Harold if they had been alive together, although somehow I do not think he would have tolerated the administrations as Lassie did.

Harold the hare was another of the animals I am indebted to for furthering my knowledge and giving me a completely new insight into the world of nature, making me want to find out more. Like many people, during my life in and around the countryside I had seen hundreds of wild animals, but never really stopping to have a good look at any one of them. It is only when you look beyond the obvious that they become interesting and then you begin to realise just how little you know and how much you want to know about them. I was determined to increase my knowledge.

Chapter 5

A change in career

Whilst at the farm in Lancashire, I had visited the auction market at Crewe on a number of occasions in pursuit of my business, both buying and selling the pedigree Friesian cattle we kept on the holding, and during the school holidays the family enjoyed the opportunity to accompany me for the ride. If the business was completed in good time, we would sometimes take the chance to make a diversion to Chester on the way home, and visit the Zoological Gardens which I must admit was as much for my benefit as theirs. A fascination for the animals kept in zoos had developed from an early age when I visited the capital on a village school outing, part of the tour being a trip to London Zoo. Since that first introduction it seemed that most holidays I had taken had been at places well within reach of a zoological park, and which was always a high priority on my itinerary.

I held Chester Zoo in high regard and had always admired the enclosures and the surroundings in which the animals were kept, as there was an extremely good and varied collection and the gardens were superb. I often thought it would be a perfect place to work in, though then, not having the faintest idea that I was soon to spend the next twenty-four years doing just that.

I was forty years old when my farming employer passed away, which meant that I would have to find an alternative means of survival. There were some opportunities offered in the agricultural field, one or two of which seemed to present security for the future, but my appetite had been whetted and I wondered about the zoological world. It was a life I had always been interested in, even though in an amateurish way, so I thought, why not invest in a stamp, write to the zoo and see if there were any vacancies, and that is exactly what I did.

It wasn't long before I had an answer to my letter, asking me to go for an interview. The ensuing visit with the director was very informal, most of the time being taken up with a tour of the gardens, including going into two areas strictly forbidden to the casual visitor, but also obviously being carefully assessed at the same time. At the end of the tour, which had taken much longer than I expected, I was asked when I could start. The question took me a little by surprise, but I replied, *"Just as soon as the farm sale has been completed and loose ends tidied up."*

There were a few raised eyebrows from the older members of my family when they were told of my intention to start a new career, thinking I was completely off my rocker moving away from farming which had been a family concern for centuries. They were somewhat placated when told that the zoo did have its own farm to produce some of the food for its inmates. To me it was a natural progression going from domestic stock to start looking after the exotic kind, and as it meant a new career the old adage saying, life begins at forty, was looking very applicable in my case.

The farm sale being duly completed, we began to pack, and discovered just how much we had accumulated over the years and we had to decide what we needed and what had to be disposed of. We were moving from a large farmhouse to a smaller three-bedroom semi, very much in reverse of our previous move. Much of the larger articles of furniture we had collected were deemed unsatisfactory and had to be left together with a snooker table, picked up at a very reasonable price, but wanting a room at least ten yards by six, which we did not have. Another problem was how to move a couple of large fish tanks, complete with fish, more items collected at the farm. This was eventually done by emptying the tanks and transporting the fish in large plastic bags at the last minute. Rocky, the parrot, of course came with us, we had got so used to his ramblings, and it was unthinkable to do otherwise. The only worrying animal predicament was Lassie. Although I would dearly have liked to take her with us, I thought it unkind to take her from a rural environment to urban surroundings. Even though house trained, as a working dog, I considered she would miss her daily rounds with the stock. With this in mind she was left with a farmer friend who already owned a sister to Lassie from the same litter and had a young family similar to our own, where I knew she would have an excellent home. I am certain, through subsequent enquires, that this proved to be the right decision for her well-being.

Our new house was situated only a hundred yards or so from the entrance to the zoo and was to be our home for the next few years, when we were then able to move into a larger detached house across the road, and even closer to work.

My position at the zoo was to be section officer. At that time the collection had two section officers, each responsible for the day to day running of the zoo, receiving their orders from the curator. The two halves of the zoo were conveniently separated by a bridle path, over which a bridge joined the sections. It was with a little trepidation I went through the time office that first Monday morning to start a new life.

I need not have worried, as the curator suggested the best method of getting to know the collection, was to work for a short term in each division, then numbering about twelve.

Actually working alongside the keepers did in fact prove to be an excellent way of getting to know not only the animals and their names, but also the keepers themselves. In many ways they were similar to the farm workers I had been used to, that they appeared to be in that type of occupation because they had a love of animals and were completely dedicated to their work, and to the animals in their care. The work involved probably attracted this sort of person not because of the financial reward, but more likely because it gave them the opportunity to get within close proximity to the animals they enjoyed being with, and looking after. The wages paid then were well below that paid in industry, the hours were longer, we worked a full six days a week, but there were few grumbles. I really appreciated those first months and the thrill it gave me to work with the many species held in the collection, something that I never lost in all the years I was at the zoo. To work in such a comprehensive collection as that held at Chester, it is a vital necessity to have a great liking and respect for the animals, and after being there for a few months, came to the conclusion that it is equally important, and probably more so for the animals, to accept and like you, which fortunately the majority seemed to do in my case.

The elephant house was the first place to familiarise myself with and that may be the reason I have a soft spot for these great animals. The elephant house was a comparatively new house, having opened about two years previously, and built by the zoo's own maintenance staff, a method used then to keep costs down to a minimum. It was a vast building with outside enclosures and, holding hippopotamus and tapirs as well as the elephants, making it one of the largest producers of manure in the grounds, and certainly requiring a bit of muscle to keep it clean and tidy.

Fortunately I had served my apprenticeship with shovel and barrow many years ago, and the barrow loads ejected by the elephants held no terrors to me.

There were many characters in the collection at the time, many persisting today, and I found that just like domestic animals and people for that matter, each individual in a group can differ enormously in their behaviour. Barbar was one such character; she was an Asian elephant, matriarch of the group and had had some training as a performer, prior to coming to the zoo. She was quite adept at using a brush when given the chance, holding it comfortably in her trunk and wielding it in the area directly ahead, she could also blow a mouth organ but those that heard it agreed it wasn't all that tuneful. She also had a wicked sense of humour. The house had a large sunken bath situated about six feet from one of the walls, and Barbar would stand against the wall waiting for some unsuspecting keeper to pass between her and the pool, then with a well placed foot she would deposit them neatly in the water. Having been forewarned of this trick, I resisted the temptation to take a short cut past her, consequently missing an early bath whilst working there.

Mr Higgins was another great character. He was a bush pig who resided in the camel house. He used to adore a little individual attention, especially at feeding times, but was renowned for his short temper. If upset in any way, his tail acted like a barometer, normally drooping, it would become erect and stick up like an aerial. This was a sign for those that knew him to get out of the way quick, those that didn't usually finished up running for dear life, and I saw a few keepers who did not know him and his habits, clambering up the cage wall with Mr Higgins' teeth clattering like castanets below them.

Across the passage from Mr Higgins was Humphrey, a Bactrian camel. He was another who could be quite grumpy at times, and keepers working with him in the paddock were normally advised to keep their barrow between him and themselves, but frequently the barrow was left behind by the keeper as he made a hasty exit with Humphrey lumbering behind. I suspect in Humphrey's case it was his idea of fun more than nastiness, but his sheer size was enough to put the wind up anybody not knowing his party trick.

Simon giving Richie, Son of George, the male giraffe, a carrot, courtesy of John Doidge

Next door we had George, the tallest giraffe seen in captivity, his size recorded in the Guinness Book of Records. He grew to his remarkable height in the zoo and once caused some confusion on the telephone switchboard by licking the overhead wires crossing the giraffe paddock, maybe getting some pleasure from the low voltage current running through them. These had to be raised a couple of feet once the problem was realised.

Alex was a capuchin monkey, a male in one of the groups we had of this South American primate. He could be handled with impunity by anybody he accepted and really enjoyed human company. When in his outside enclosure, his eyesight was so good, he could pick out anybody he knew out of a crowd of hundreds, screaming excitedly to draw attention to the fact he had seen you. He would also tease visitors, especially those wearing spectacles, by hanging onto the cage where people could reach his extended hand, and then his long prehensile tail would shoot out to pick off the glasses from their nose. These seemed to have a special fascination for Alex, and a special notice had to be put on the cage warning of the danger, and so depriving him of his little trick.

All the bears were past masters at encouraging visitors to feed them, standing high on their hind legs, and waving for any food being carried. Their begging was so successful that rations could be cut by half in the summer when the majority of people came. This feeding was frowned upon, so we asked visitors not to do so because we fed all the animals a balanced diet formulated to keep them healthy, and in good condition, and whilst most of the food visitors gave was wholesome, certain things that were given had entirely the opposite effect than that we were trying to achieve. We often said that if people could see the result of wrongful and excessive feeding the following morning, it would help us greatly to stop the suffering it can cause.

Sammy was yet another to be remembered. He was a Californian sea lion, usually to be found in the sea lion pool, but well capable of scaling the surrounding fence which he often did, as soon as he spotted the keeper coming with a bucket of fish at feeding times. The sea lions were fed at regular times during the day, and watches could be set by their anticipation of this event which could be seen by their mounting excitement as the minutes ticked by, their heads bobbing in the water and looking in the direction they knew the food was coming from. Feeding was always a popular event, and the largest crowds would be seen around the pool to see these active mammals in action.

It would be wrong not to include Tim, the male of a pair of Bengal tigers at the zoo, amongst these great characters. He would delight in drawing a large crowd to his enclosure with his loud roars, and then without warning, turn and spray the unsuspecting group with a well directed jet of warm fluid, an action that seemed to give him some perverse pleasure.

There was a large collection of the anthropoid apes, and everyone as individual as one would expect our closest relations to be. We had two pairs of gorilla, Jason and Gogal from the western species and Mukisi and Noelle representing the eastern family. Paul and Jimmy were two orang-utans and there was a large colony of chimpanzee, too many to list by name, but every one a character in their own right.

Like the bears, most of the large apes were quite clever at persuading our visitors to part with some of their lunch, which again we attempted to discourage. A lot of time and energy went into preparing a balanced diet for them, to keep the animals in peak condition, and the extra feeding caused many dietary problems. At one time it seemed an almost traditional practice when visiting a zoo, to feed the inmates, a trend which I am pleased to say I have seen reversed, due to a more educated public visiting. This has also meant the animals living a longer healthier life and resulted in them having a far better breeding record by not consuming quantities of unnecessary extra food.

Chapter 6

Some moving moments

I was fortunate being at the zoo in the boom years during the late 1960's and early 70s when over a million visitors came through the gates annually. The income generated from those numbers helped greatly in the expansion of the zoo onto our existing farmland, and also with building the collection.

In the past, many zoos could have been accused of being animal consumers rather than conservers, exploiting their collections for monetary gain, but things were changing. There was a general awareness in the zoological world that animals could not be continually collected from the wild just for exhibition, and they would have to breed their own replacements, putting the emphasis on the world's rarer species, with a longer term view to release captive bred stock back to strengthen the generally declining stocks in the wild.

Towards this end, the National Federation of Zoological Gardens of Great Britain and Ireland was formed and co-operation between zoos became more commonplace. Where previously surplus animals were sold or exchanged for others of similar value it became the practice to move them around to complete pairs or breeding groups and placed in conditions that suited their particular species best. Co-operation was further enhanced with the formation of the Joint Management of Species Group, now expanded to incorporate many of the leading continental zoos. By this time I had been very lucky, due to various circumstances, to have become curator at Chester and fortunate to have been concerned with the above group from its outset. Meetings of the Joint Management committee were held regularly and hosted in turn by member zoos, various representatives of the group being responsible for keeping studbooks of the various rarer species and advising in the policy of keeping that particular species. The group in general were working to do everything possible for the furtherance of every endangered species kept in the federation zoos.

I travelled hundreds of miles up and down the country to attend meetings, most of which were extremely informative and invaluable in helping me to keep in touch with all the new developments in the zoological world. I also travelled hundreds of miles during my years at Chester, transporting dozens of mammals, birds and reptiles to and from the zoo.

People going about their normal business, driving on roads up and down the country, could have little knowledge of what they were passing in lorries, vans and trailers. When I was moving stock, I always preferred to have a plain vehicle, as if a stop was necessary, a van with Chester Zoo emblazoned on the side was sure to attract the inquisitive to enquire what was being carried, and that usually led to, *"Can I have a look?"* which was not always convenient.

I will forever remember my first animal transportation. We had a single female ostrich in the collection and were looking for a male companion for her, and were offered a male free of charge from a collection in the West Country. I was given the chance to collect him; with the chance of seeing a zoo I had not up to then visited. The journey down was without incident, and the bird duly loaded with an ominous sounding warning that it was prone now and again to having a fit, when it would run around in circles with his head under his wing. However, as I was already there and there was nothing to lose, the return journey was begun with a premonition that my travelling companion and I should expect something out the ordinary. The ostrich was travelling in a custom built crate on the back of an open truck, and for the first fifty miles or so all was quiet, except for the odd movement behind us. Then a more violent movement was felt at the rear. Finding a convenient spot, I stopped the vehicle and my colleague and I went to investigate and there, as described, was the ostrich coming out from what I surmised was a fit, with his head somewhere adjacent to where his tail should be. As soon as he realised we were there, looking at him, he stood in a more natural position giving a rather quizzical look from a height of about seven feet. We continued on our way and just north of Birmingham a similar occurrence happened, this time when we looked, he was again laid down, head in similar position, but also looking quite comfortable, so we carried on to Chester. When we then opened the crate he was still in the same position, looking very comfortable, but also dead. The subsequent post mortem showed that nothing we could have done would have prevented his death; even so I did feel a little guilty and wondered if we hadn't attempted the move, whether he would have still been running around, albeit with his head tucked under his wing. Happily that proved to be the only casualty I experienced in the dozens of moves I made in the following years.

If coming from abroad, many of the animals travelled by air and therefore these collections would be made at airports, where we would gather an assortment of creatures from sources around the world. These had a habit of arriving at unsociable hours and to save any further stress quite often meant meeting the planes in the late evening and into the small hours. There was also a little apprehension on these occasions as numerous forms and licences were required, and custom regulations so strict, that it was not unusual to get through the formalities without some problem cropping up.

One such assignment necessitated collecting a consignment of rock hyrax from South Africa. All the appropriate papers were in order, but a customs official was rather worried about the description. 'Rock Rabbits' was written on the crates. This apparently is a local name given to the hyrax, and written on the boxes by the consignee unaware of the problem it would cause, as then rabbits required a special licence to import, which of course I did not have or need. He did not seem inclined to accept my explanation that hyrax were not rabbits, moreover they were not even rodents even though in appearance they could have been either, and when I further explained that their nearest relative in the animal kingdom was an elephant, (which is true) he was rather suspicious that I was trying to pull the wool over his eyes.

It was morning before the hyrax were finally released into my custody, after contacting the Ministry of Agriculture for confirmation that the information I had given them was correct. I accepted the apologies for the delay and the invitation for breakfast before travelling home with the animals.

It was at the same airport that a pair of kudu arrived from Munich Zoo, and which were to be delivered to our quarantine premises situated at Prenton, close to Birkenhead. This time the name kudu had been confused with pudu found on the category one endangered species list, and I was told I did not have the necessary papers to import this particular species. Fortunately, I was able to convince them that a pudu was in fact a small South American deer, whereas the kudu was a large African antelope, and a quick look at the animals in question would soon clear any doubt. I was soon on the road after this slight delay, driving towards the Wirral and yet again, through the early morning hours, which was somewhat recompensed by the sighting of two badgers foraging on the side of the motorway.

Although this kind of experience did happen to be an exception, rather than the rule, we must accept the regulations and rules are there for our protection, and very necessary if we are to keep a record of the import and export of animals with any health risk.

Once, delivering a large cat we had exchanged for a pair of Andean condors, travelling through the midlands I pulled into a garage for fuel. The attendant having filled the tank, asked if there was anything else I required, and I resisted the temptation to say if he wished he could go round the back to see if the Jaguar wanted filling up as well. Another time in the same area I was collecting an Ankole bull from a private collector, this large member of the cattle family had a pair of horns almost the width of the metal trailer we had taken to transport him in. As he had never been fastened up and unused to a halter he was left loose in the trailer, and as he moved and turned around, the ensuing noise rather resembled a Trinidad steel band without the melody. I could imagine some of the people we passed on the journey home wondering what on earth we were carrying.

The smaller animals usually posed no problem and were not difficult to manage as they were generally quite happy to curl up and go to sleep in their travelling crates and take little interest in the proceedings, though I do recollect a consignment of locust escaping from their packaging and attempting to colonise the local railway station goods department. Some of the larger animals however, could prove rather more difficult, for instance a large orang-utan or chimpanzee could stand upright in its crate rocking from first one side and then to the other, which could have quite an alarming effect on a vehicle, and was rather like trying to control a small boat on a rough sea.

In the later years, modern drugs made the whole

procedure of moving larger animals much easier and also far less traumatic for the animal concerned. The subject could be tranquillised in its own enclosure, then when the drug was reversed and the animal woken up minutes later, it was safely in the crate ready to go. In between however, there could be some quite heavy lifting by those involved.

No animal would be moved whilst completely sedated, in the event of a slight sedation to calm a nervous one it would be kept under constant supervision on the road.

I once moved a pair of polar bear from a Midlands Zoo, both of which were sedated to facilitate the move. The female wasn't too bad and relatively easily lifted by about six willing helpers, but the male was an entirely different proposition, as he must have weighed about twelve hundredweight and looked twice the size laid down than he did standing up. Loading him was finally accomplished by the same helpers, this time not nearly so willing, with much huffing and puffing and advice (mainly ignored) coming from others looking on. After reversing the drugs and loading the bears onto the wagon the journey home was a formality and both bears came out the crates under their own steam, far easier than they had gone in.

The motorway network has proved to be a great advantage especially with the larger loads, as prior to these being built, the journeys were slower, and should an adult giraffe have to be moved, the route had to be carefully planned in advance, as a fifteen foot high crate on a wagon meant bridges under eighteen feet had to be avoided, if we were to arrive home safely.

We also experienced a few crazy moments when moving various animals, a male zebra once causing an amusing episode when representatives from another zoo came to collect it. zebras, especially males, are not noted for being the most co-operative of animals, and this one decided it was not going to be the one to change that reputation. After using various means of persuasion, lasting far longer than we had anticipated, it was safely inside the travelling crate they had brought to collect it. Then we had to get it on board their waiting wagon. It was gradually eased into a position where our small crane could lift it onto the truck; cables were attached to all four corners of the crate and the driver given instructions to lift away. Unfortunately, when he took the strain, the crate lifted, but the base with the zebra standing on it didn't, that stayed where it was on the ground. A number of voices in unison rather excitedly told the driver of the crane to drop it quick. Luckily we had another suitable crate on site and were able to transfer the animal from one to the other with a minimum of fuss, allowing our colleagues to go home with our crate and minus a heap of firewood.

When another zoo came to collect a young hippopotamus, we were expecting some difficulties, but certainly had not anticipated the one that actually happened. On their arrival I did express my doubts as to whether the crate they had brought was strong enough for the job in question, but they assured me that it had recently been used in the collection of another hippo. Our young male, Harry, had been born in the zoo and was about eighteen months old and probably weighed about a ton. One of the problems we had was separating him from his mother, because she was being very protective towards him as our adult male was beginning to look upon Harry as a rival, and chased him at every opportunity. Harry was therefore staying very close to his mother and followed her so closely, it was difficult to part them. It was hoped to complete this manoeuvre inside the hippo house, leaving the adult pair in one enclosure, and young Harry next door in another. After about half a dozen passes between the two enclosures and a few raised voices, which always seemed to accompany these occasions, the slide was finally slotted home and the three animals in the position required. Our friend's crate was then slid into a space in the outside enclosure, against the door through which we hoped to persuade Harry to go. The crate was held there by a number of willing hands and one or two slightly nervous ones, and I stationed myself on top, holding the slide in readiness to drop it immediately the hippo entered it, or if he should enter it, because there was some doubt whether he would move at all. Then it all happened at once. Harry, probably confused with all the previous moves, probably thought mother was outside, and the moment the enclosure door opened he saw daylight and was at the front of the crate in a split second. I dropped the slide into place and we had him where we wanted him. Harry, however, thought different. He reared on his hind legs, and his impact with the top of the crate caused that to part company with the sides, and the whole lot collapsed in a heap on the ground, and Harry was at liberty in the paddock. During the next few seconds, I am certain half a dozen sprint records and a couple of high jump records were unofficially broken, and I recall thinking, it's moments like this when you find who your friends are. Luckily nobody was hurt, and the three hippos were reunited to let them settle down again, and our colleagues told to go home empty handed and return at a later date with a stronger crate. That time the operation went according to plan and Harry found a new home and a befitting mate.

Chapter 7

Quarantine

The zoo owned its own quarantine station at Prenton in the Wirral. The appropriate authorities demanded, and rightly so, that most imported stock had to be subjected to a predetermined period isolated from any other animals. Our premises were mainly intended for ungulates which at that time had to stay in such isolation for twelve calendar months. Carnivores, which were subject to a six-month quarantine period, were normally housed in an approved area within the zoo. These periods were essential to check that no disease or parasite was brought into the country to infect domestic stock and if anything untoward should be found, be effectively treated before the animal was allowed to leave the designated area.

It was shortly after starting at the zoo, when I made my first acquaintance with Roy, our man at Prenton. Roy was then getting on in years, but still quite active and certainly not looking ahead to retirement. He actually lived about a mile away from the station but I got the impression he was never far away from it, as whenever you made a call, he was usually there to answer it. He was a real character but his qualities as a stock man could not be faulted, even if sometimes I wondered how he wasn't injured taking the chances he did with the animals he happened to be looking after. He would walk into the apartment with the stock, and they just stood and stared at his apparent effrontery. I was never sure whether he lived a charmed life or had the attributes of Dr Doolittle.

Roy seldom had any time off during the week, but if he did, and when he was on holiday, I generally stood in for him to feed and care for any animals there at the time. To keep the place ticking over if nothing was being quarantined; during the winter some of the animals more susceptible to the cold, such as the Arabian gazelles, would be taken there from the zoo to take advantage of the cosy quarters.

My first introduction to moving animals from quarantine involved crating eight wildebeests, which having completed their year at Prenton, were bound for a zoo down south. The object of the exercise was to separate the animals one at a time, and then funnel it down a narrow passage, and from there into its travelling crate. That is the theory part and that usually sounds a simple operation, in practice if the animal doesn't co-operate then patience is essential if you do not want it to become too excited to manage. Frequently you will find that one animal does not want to be separated from its own kind, and no matter how many times they pass an open door, they either do not see it or do not want to go through it. True to form, Roy was in the thick of it, trying to persuade awkward individuals to go through a door they were not used to using. Perseverance eventually prevailed and gradually one by one they were put in their separate crates, with Roy frequently disappearing to put the kettle on to make a cup of tea, to which he seemed to have a particular addiction.

We had a gantry in the yard which held a series of pulleys powered by a winch that had been acquired from the local docks, and this was used to lift the filled crates one at a time into the air, allowing the wagon to reverse under, whilst the animal was then lowered into its travelling position. This part of the proceedings went off according to plan and all eight were sheeted down and on their way, just in time for us to catch the local fish and chip shop before it closed for a slightly delayed lunch, together with a cup of tea brewed by

Roy. We then left him with his memories of wildebeest and quite a lot of cleaning up.

Not long after the wildebeest went, four giraffes were accepted to quarantine for another collection. These had been collected in Kenya and travelled by ship to Bristol, from where they were transported by road to our quarters.

It was evening by the time they arrived with us at Prenton, fortunately, a fine night and as it was summer we had a certain amount of daylight to unload, but even then it was dark by the time the operation was completed. The two lorries, each carrying two crates, aroused some interest as they parked on the road outside the quarters and the usual small crowd gathered to watch the proceedings, especially when some of the sheeting was removed to allow the giraffes some fresh air, and a look round their surroundings. They behaved remarkably well during the unloading, even though two were a little reluctant to leave the crates that had been their homes for a couple of weeks or so. They soon appeared to be at home in their new quarters and eating a variety of food that had been placed there in readiness.

Once they had settled and accepted their surrounds and our presence, closer inspection showed they had a profusion of ticks feeding on them. Then having been looked at by a ministry veterinary inspector, he suggested that the ticks could be eliminated by dipping the animals using a proprietary sheep dip, though conveniently disappearing before mentioning how this should be accomplished. Not having a suitable bath for a giraffe, we compromised using a stirrup pump which somehow had survived from war time duties to spray the sheep dip over the giraffes, soaking them from head to foot. It was quite a hit and miss operation each time we did it and not at all appreciated by the animals, and by the time they had got used to it was no longer necessary because the ticks had all succumbed. The treatment, besides having the desired effect on the ticks also seemed to improve the coats on the giraffes, and another benefit meant the walls were also washed and disinfected with the excess dip that missed the animals.

As it happened, I was invited the following winter to speak at a ladies' luncheon meeting, and a small diversion meant I could call in at the quarantine station and have a quick look at the giraffes. They had by this time become quite friendly and after feeding them a few carrots, I was assured everything was in order and I continued on my way. We were getting well through the lunch and about to start on the dessert course, and I was trying to think of an appropriate opening remark, when right in the centre of the top table between myself and our lady chairman, there appeared a big, shiny, black flea. Before I could identify the species, a couple of good hops put it out of sight, and somebody probably acquired a lodger. It was obvious to me that it was also seen by madam chairman, whose sudden look of horror was sufficient proof that she too had noticed the intruder. Nothing was said at the time, but after the meeting our host asked me if I had seen the flea, which of course I confirmed. She then went to some length to explain that prior to coming to the meeting she had been playing with her dogs and must have collected the flea from them. I accepted her explanation gratefully and failed to mention that I too could easily have transported it, as prior to coming to the meeting it could have been picked up from the straw, or alternatively been some exotic species from the giraffes, though that would have been extremely unlikely after the washing they went through.

When it came to the giraffes turn to be moved, we were faced with another problem. They had done so well their heights had increased by as much as four feet. This increase meant that their heads were above the height of the doors and as they were disinclined to lower their heads, they were reluctant to leave the quarters housing them. Eventually they had to be persuaded by us standing on ladders by the door, and pushing their necks down so they could see where we wanted them to go. Luckily, Roy had got them quiet enough to allow this sort of treatment. Loading the wagons was just the opposite of unloading them, again one at a time, with Roy operating the winch, lifting each one in turn, to allow the wagon to reverse under. When the third was in the air, the shout to lower was met with no response. Roy, having tired of the time the driver took to shunt his wagon into position, had gone to put the kettle on.

Next to be held in quarantine were a number of markhor, also being held for another collection. The markhor, a wild goat from the Himalayas proved to be quite lively. They were held in the smaller of the two animal sheds which had four compartments separated by eight foot high partitions and serviced from a common passage running the length of the building. The partitions proved to be no barrier for the agile goats and they exchanged compartments at will and to make things more manageable, the interior walls were extended with mesh to the roof. Things went well for a while and they stayed where they were put, then just four days before Christmas, there was a call from Roy to say one of the markhor had got out. Apparently it slipped past him when he was feeding, and inadvertently he had also left the safety gate open. Fortunately, the sheep sized goat was not particularly dangerous but nevertheless it was a serious matter having a quarantined animal at liberty and it had to be reported immediately to the authorities. A 'safari' party was quickly organised and transported to Prenton where we arrived at the same time as some of the local police force. The sergeant enquired as to which way the animal had disappeared, and when told, suggested it was probably as well it hadn't gone in the opposite direction as it might have then ended up in somebody's freezer. The next two days proved to be quite entertaining, even if somewhat serious, and I am sure the police who were present during the operation enjoyed the whole episode, which was entirely different to their normal routine. The radios they carried were a great asset in following our prey, which according to the many calls from householders in the area, seemed to be travelling like the cartoon roadrunner. Walls and fences round Prenton were no obstacle to an animal used to negotiating mountains in the Himalayas. When we knocked on one door to ask a gentleman if we could follow it into his garden where we had seen it go, he replied that he had just come in from there and hadn't seen it, but in there it was stood, on the bedroom windowsill which couldn't have been more than three inches wide. One look at us, armed with nets, was sufficient, and away it went. One leap took it from the window ledge onto the garage roof, another into next door's garden from whence it took a row of fences like an Olympic hurdler and disappeared from sight. Two streets away an old lady answered our next request to hunt in her garden by asking what we were looking for. The officer accompanying me said, *"A goat,"* I think perhaps the lady may have been rather deaf because as she mumbled to herself, *"a ghost,"* she was rapidly disappearing into the safety of the house. The same officer said to me some time later that he had seen parts of the area he never knew existed, and it would be possible to hide a herd of goats in some of the gardens we visited, never mind a single one. The only time during the first day we came anywhere near catching it was when we cornered it in a cul-de-sac but on closing in, it ran round the three walls ahead of us as though it was practising on the wall of death, jumping well over our heads and vanished once again into the approaching darkness. It was at this point it was proposed that we abandoned the search until early the following morning.

Next day, the word had got around the district that a wild animal was on the prowl and simultaneous calls from well intentioned people had the goat running around the local golf course and heading down the road towards the Mersey tunnel, about four miles apart. It was finally located browsing in a shrubbery not far from where we had lost it the evening before, and had probably spent the night there and obviously recharged its batteries, as it cleared a six foot fence on seeing us and we lost it again.

Time passed quickly as we followed up calls, and we were beginning to wonder whether we would still be looking on Christmas Eve, when we got another positive sighting. Quickly reaching the area, we spotted its head held high happily trotting down the road in front of us. Suddenly turning, it went through a garden gate and straight through the front door of the house conveniently open at the time. By then we were close on its heels and were quickly admitted by the lady of the house, and the door was shut. It was followed into the lounge where three young boys were sat on the settee watching the television, and so engrossed that they hardly took their eyes off it as the goat did three laps around them. The markhor was quickly overpowered and transported back to the quarantine station by a bunch of mortals not as well equipped to cover the territory as it was. It certainly gave a good account of itself and gave us a sometimes frustrating and sometimes hilarious two days, at a time when we could have done well without it.

Charlie kudu was one of the pair mentioned in an earlier chapter also spending his first year in England at Prenton, together with his mate, Zoe, and they matured there together. kudu's are not noted for their tractability, tending to be rather shy creatures, but Charlie was just the opposite. Full of confidence, as soon as you entered the house he would come across to greet you looking for the expected titbit which of course was always forthcoming, and he knew it, but you had to be aware of his long, sharp, curving horns, which he was keen to try out on any yielding object. Zoe was a far more reserved and gentle animal and would wait patiently for the food to be brought to her.

It was later in the year when I noticed holes appearing in the plasterboard ceiling that doubled as insulation, and on mentioning it to Roy, I was told Charlie Boy was growing up fast, and in attempting to mate with Zoe, his horns were hitting the roof. Charlie, by this time, was getting the long spiral horns associated with the species and when rearing on his hind legs the tips of his horns must have been about ten feet from the ground. He was also successful in his mating attempts, and we had a calf born to the pair after they had completed their quarantine and come down to Chester. The calf being a young male, I subsequently reared on the bottle due to the inability of the female to feed it on this occasion.

A few years' later new regulations regarding quarantine were drawn up by the Ministry concerned, which made it impossible to have the larger animals there and the housing was redesigned to hold smaller stock and birds which then required a thirty-five day quarantine period when coming in from abroad. I think it also cut out much of the excitement the larger animals generated, and whilst the premises were still important to the zoo it certainly did not create the character of some of those entertained there in the past.

Chapter 8

Across the water

Although most of the animal transportations between foreign zoos are now done by air which is far quicker than vehicular travel, there are still many moves the old fashioned way, involving road and sea journeys.

Both methods require the safe confinement of the animal(s) concerned, but generally airlines are far more meticulous in their requirements for the construction and size of the crates used to carry them. There are guidelines available from the airline authorities for the manufacture of crates to suit all species likely to be carried, and providing these are strictly adhered to, there is usually no problem when taking animals to an airport for export. But making custom built crates of this type and quality is now quite an expensive business and would add greatly to the cost of moving stock. For instance, should you have six antelope to transport, making the crates for these could cost more than moving the same animals in a trailer, so it could make sense economically to use the latter method, and in my experience I consider they also travel better with less stress than they do when individually boxed.

At the zoo, as well as a trailer, we had two vans, one small and one large, specially adapted and licensed to carry animals destined to go into quarantine or sent abroad. Travelling by road to deliver or collect animals abroad, also had the added bonus of being able to visit other zoos, seeing how their methods contrast with our own, and compare like exhibits together with a good chance of learning something new, and also gave the chance of a little sightseeing.

I managed to see a number of the continental zoos using the excuse of collecting and delivering stock, and also added to my circle of friends.

One of the earlier trips I made was to Copenhagen, to collect a pair of young polar bears which had been bred in the zoo there. On this occasion I was driving the larger of the two vans with Chester Zoo well advertised on the sides, and holding two large crates for the bears on the return journey. All the appropriate paper work had been done in advance, together with obtaining the approval to quarantine the animals in an enclosure within the zoo for the six month regulatory period necessary for carnivores. This also meant that they would be on view to our visitors during the time they were in isolation, and as they were well away from other stock and zoo bred, there was little likelihood of any disease. The journey first meant a drive to Harwich, despite many trips into East Anglia, I have yet to find an easy route, then pick up a ferry to Esbjerg followed by another drive across the mainland and the two islands of Denmark, including another ferry trip, before reaching Copenhagen. On reaching the zoo itself, it would be ungenerous to fault the hospitality, meals were provided and I was booked into an extremely comfortable hotel in the centre of the city. As a special treat the following day, I was invited to accompany the director of the zoo to a special lunch at a nearby hostelry which included a generous supply of a local lager, together with an undefined number of glasses of schnapps. After imbibing I was rather pleased I did not have to drive anywhere, and could quite easily have gone to sleep for the rest of the afternoon, however, I did recover sufficiently to take in some of the city nightlife later in the evening.

The following morning, our two young bears were duly loaded for their journey to England, which on my part was started a little reluctantly, and the intention to get back there someday firmly implanted in my mind.

I intended to make the return trip to Esbjerg in time to catch the D.F.D.S Dana Anglia, which was a new ship recently commissioned, and the one I had travelled over on. This was accomplished with time to spare and I was one of the first vehicles to arrive on the quay. Having survived all the custom formalities, I was waiting at the dockside with only a single truck in front, and was approached by a ships official who enquired what I may be carrying, obviously interested in the zoo's logo on the side of the van. He radioed my answer of two polar bears to the bridge and back came the response, *"Well he's not bringing them on my ship."* I was a little put out by this reaction to say the least, but then immediately put at ease when told, *"I wouldn't take much notice of that, the Captain is a mite uneasy about carrying animals on board because we had a travelling circus on last week, and they let a couple of tigers out on the lorry deck."* I need not have worried as I was able to assure him that the bears were safely crated and I wouldn't be letting them out for exercise, so it wasn't very long before the bears and I were aboard, and receiving five star treatment. I should also mention that crossing the North Sea on that occasion was the roughest I have ever made and forty-foot seas were encountered. Even so, we were only an hour late arriving at Harwich, and I am pleased to say I was not one of the unfortunates aboard who could not find the stomach to take advantage of the superb food on offer, and not one of the many I saw, continually making a beeline for the washroom.

The custom officials at Harwich were reluctant to search inside the crates for contraband and happy to take my word that I wasn't carrying anything I shouldn't, and I was soon on my way to Chester.

Although they travelled well and matured into superb animals, the story had a tragic end, both bears dying prematurely. The female was the first to go, in ideal polar bear conditions. Following a long spell of frosty weather, their enclosure pond was covered by a thick layer of ice, except for an area of about five yards across, kept clear by the bear's activities and they could clearly be seen swimming around beneath the ice, exploring the extent of the pool. On one particular day we had snow and in almost blizzard conditions, both bears were seen to be chasing about, seemingly enjoying the arctic weather, and when one was missed, a search showed she was drowned not far from the hole in the ice. The post mortem examination showed she had in fact been drowned and we had to assume that in chasing around she had slipped, temporarily stunning herself before entering the water, being such a strong swimmer, there was no other explanation.

The male drowned eighteen months later in totally different conditions. This time it was mid summer in front of a large crowd of visitors. He too was swimming in the pool, playing with another female on a hot day, and must have been inhaling the moment she pushed his head under the water, some of which entered his lungs and killed him. It is not often you hear of bears being drowned, and we were unlucky having two within two years. These examples led us to wonder just how many similar cases happen in the wild which we would never hear about, and a question that will never be answered satisfactorily.

Two trips to Switzerland had much longer lasting results. The first trip entailed collecting a Spectacled Bear from another collection in the UK to take to Zurich, and bring back a pair of Asiatic lions. Travelling this time with Jim, a colleague at the zoo and co-driver, we drove across France hoping to reach Zurich in the late evening, accommodation already being booked in advance. But a snag was encountered at the border town of Basle. We arrived just in time to find the French veterinary official had gone home for his tea and was not available to inspect the bear and stamp our certificate necessary to allow us to leave the country. That meant we had to make an unscheduled stop overnight in *'no mans land,'* on the French side of the border.

Usually equipped for most emergencies on these trips, I had an air mattress and sleeping bag and after a meal and drink in a café recommended by a lorry driver, which in itself was an experience, settled down for a night's sleep in the back of the van, with the bear for company. Jim had the cab for his bedroom whilst I had a narrow space between the crate holding the bear and the side of the van. That space must have been a little too narrow, as during the night a searching claw managed to puncture the mattress, and the only air left was in the pillow. The remainder of the night could have been more comfortable, and I remember thinking the bears breath could also have been a little sweeter.

On the return journey we had a similar experience at the same crossing, and involving the same official, and we had a two hour wait until he could be located. I am not sure where he had been, but I suspect out to lunch, as when he finally appeared, the strong smell of garlic on this breath made him a far worse proposition to face than the bear, and that was bad enough.

The second trip to Switzerland involved equines, and as the restrictions for moving horses were not quite as stringent, a Land Rover and trailer was the choice of transport. This time I was supported by a keeper and co-driver, Martin, plus another colleague, Derryck, who offered his assistance in exchange for the ride and in fact became a useful member of the team acting as interpreter and extra driver, as well as being excellent company.

Again we managed to find a load to take out as well as the intended load to we were to bring back. Through the connection with the Joint Management group, I had promised to collect a pair of Prezewalski horses from a collection down south to take to the private collection near Basle, where we were also to pick up a trio of Onager wild asses to bring back to Chester. Having successfully accomplished the first part, loading the horses, we arrived at Dover only to find we were one certificate short and had to travel back inland to an equine centre for a veterinary inspection, and the appropriate piece of paper to allow us to continue on the way. Fortunately the ferries run frequently from Dover across the channel to Calais and this hitch did not cause too much of a delay. We had no further problems with that load and none until it came to loading the Onagers. A description of the overindulgence of food and drink between our arrival and departure on the Swiss side of Basle, and provided by our generous host, is probably best omitted, but probably left us not in the best of condition to contemplate the job in hand.

The Onagers were housed in a part of the collection which couldn't be reached by the vehicle, so they had to be put into individual crates which then had to be manhandled from their enclosure into the loading area one by one. Onagers are never the easiest of animals to deal with and these proved to be no exception to the rule, and following an early start the whole operation took up the best part of the morning. Eventually carried out to the satisfaction of everyone concerned, the three Onagers were safely transferred to our trailer without any harm done to either them or ourselves, though during the process a few flying hooves in our direction had been a threat. We said goodbye to

Switzerland after another satisfying lunch and checking that the animals had settled down in the trailer, and with three drivers taking spells at the wheel, we were able to drive practically non-stop throughout the night, clearing customs in record time. Seeing the white cliffs at Dover is always a welcoming sight and once on British soil it is easy to think you are home, but it is still a long haul to Chester. Even so, the whole trip was completed in just under eighteen hours, and the Onagers were eating Cheshire grass the morning after grazing in Switzerland.

A far more successful journey than the first one I had made to collect an ostrich entailed making a trip to southern Ireland. I had been in the habit of contacting local businesses to sponsor some of the collecting trips, and been fortunate in having good relations with a local Land Rover agent who provided a vehicle on a number of occasions. This time I also persuaded a ferry company to give a free crossing to Ireland, and in return they were able to get a few publicity shots of the important passenger. A round trip was made out from Holyhead to Dun Laoghaire followed by a pleasant drive down to Cork. Ireland is a lovely country and the people so friendly it is always a delight to go there and it surprises me that there are so few tourists taking the opportunities that Ireland affords. Having made this journey before, it was a simple matter to locate Fota Island where a rather different kind of wildlife park is situated and renew my acquaintance with the director there. The animals and birds in the park are given as much freedom as the species allow, many roaming loose within the confines of the gardens, and it seems to work extremely well in the mild climate which probably benefits from the gulf stream. Walking round the park it pays to keep ones eyes open as macaws, monkeys and lemurs are to be seen in the trees overhead and there are kangaroos and wallabies running about at ground level. As always happens, the time to go home comes all too quickly and we had to load a somewhat reluctant bird into our trailer. It was a relatively simple matter to get the big bird into its shed where it was used to going for food, but an entirely different matter to get it out and walk up the short ramp and into the compartment for the journey home. Eventually, with the help of a few plywood panels and a bucketful of tempting food, it was loaded and I left southern Ireland this time by a different route to get the ferry from Rosslare to Fishguard where I had arranged to meet the photographer from the ferry company.

I have found from experience on these occasions the usual requirements for a publicity shot are a camera, a pretty girl and a compliant animal. The first two were waiting on the dock and the third safely fastened up in the trailer, and the immediate problem was how to get the three parts of the equation together. The cameraman wondered if the trailer door would open and I agreed it would, but then couldn't guarantee the ostrich would be in a position to take a picture, and would be more likely to be legging it towards the distant hills. Fortunately the trailer did have a double door, so I suggested, with the aid of a pair of steps for our pretty girl and the top door open, both heads would be about the same height and the ostrich may just be persuaded to take some food from her. That is where the compliant animals comes in. After setting up the steps, and posing the model, the bird wanted nothing to do with her or the food offered, and stubbornly refused to move from the front to the rear of the trailer. After a while and a little gentle prodding from the front, it finally condescended to walk to the rear of the trailer and rather ungratefully pecked the girl instead of the lettuce she was holding. By now the pretty girl was getting more reluctant than the bird, but finally due to another misdirected peck, which fortunately hit the lettuce instead of the arm holding it, the cameraman was able to get the shot he had in mind, the door was quickly closed, and any vision of Rod Hull's Emu being emulated did not quite materialise.

The final result of this trip proved to be well rewarded as together with the male, we had the pair produce eggs, and successfully reared the resultant chicks.

Chapter 9

"Hello is that zoo"

The telephone was a marvellous invention enabling you to speak to your neighbour or friends and colleagues across the other side of the world with ease. It was an essential piece of equipment in the zoo which had its own switchboard and telephone system throughout the grounds, combined with a radio structure to cover any emergency, and it would have been inconceivable to think of running the business without it.

However, telephones do have drawbacks, especially the zoo phones which seem to attract a number of funny calls. You could be certain that all the lines would be busy on the first day of April, all fools day, when the operator would have anything up to a thousand calls to deal with. Most would realise they had been duped as soon as the operator said "Chester Zoo", but it was amazing just how many would go blithely on and ask for Mr Lion, Mr Links, Mrs Peacock, Mrs Parrot and some cleverer ones like; Mrs C Lion, Mr G Raffe and Mr L E Fant and even more elaborate ones wanting a monkey wrench or a carburettor for a jaguar or could we speak to the leader of the beaver pack.

It was not only on April Fools day that the funny calls came in, I had many over the years.

One lady rang to ask if I had any ideas why her pet rabbit did not breed as she thought it quite natural with that species to do so. Following questions on housing and feeding for which the answers seemed to be perfectly adequate, I suggested it may be prudent to change the buck. Amazingly then it transpired that she only had one rabbit, how she expected it to breed I am not certain, but she did go on to explain that she also kept hens and didn't have a cockerel, and they were laying eggs.

Sometimes I got the impression that the caller may be lonely and just wanted somebody to talk to, as many of the enquiries were not really of any concern to me but I did try to help whenever possible.

One caller asked if we had lost a penguin and when I said no, the caller got quite indignant and told me one had just flown over their house, and it must have been one of ours because it came from our direction. When I mentioned that penguins do not fly, our caller then wanted to know what it was. I said not having seen it I did not know, but if it was described I would hazard a guess. Well it was black and white I was told, and our caller appeared to be satisfied when I said it most likely would have been a magpie. A magpie on another occasion was described as having all the colours of the rainbow, and from the description sounded like some tropical parrot, but further investigation proved otherwise.

Kinkajous, one of the little green men.

A caller from Ellesmere Port implied that a little green man was taking the tops off her milk bottles and drinking some of the contents, and was insistent that she had seen him doing it on more than one occasion. I was a little amused at her description, but also a little worried, because she sounded so genuine and I could offer no explanation other than, as I did not believe in alien beings, perhaps one of her neighbours was the owner of a pet squirrel monkey, the nearest living thing that seemed to fit the description. But as it happened, about two weeks later, I received another call from the same area to collect an animal caught in the garden shed. This turned out to be a kinkajou, which rather resembled our previous caller's visitor, so perhaps the identity of our pseudo Martian had been exposed. We assumed the Kinkajou had been a sailor's pet and slipped off a ship in port at the time, and as it could therefore have been an illegal immigrant, had to be put into quarantine for six months prior to joining a group we had in the collection.

We were regularly blamed when people lost goldfish from their garden ponds, saying they had seen one of our big birds flying away after a spell of fishing. The culprits usually turned out to be herons which are quite prevalent in the area, and frequently come into the zoo at night in the hope of finding a few fish left by the penguins and sea lions. It could be that the callers were hoping for a little compensation for feeding our birds.

One morning, a lady called to say there was a chimpanzee in an apple tree at the bottom of her garden and would we please come and catch it. I thought it extremely unlikely as we knew all the private collections in the area and the only chimpanzees about were those in the zoo, and none of those were missing. However, the lady sounded very rational and also very adamant that it was a chimp, so I told her we would be there in a few minutes. Quickly gathering together some capture equipment and Alan, a keeper who happened to be handy at the time; we were at her house within just ten minutes of receiving the call.

"It's still in the tree," we were told. 'My husband saw it first, when he was going to work, but you can't just see it from here you will have to come up into the bedroom.' I had a rather uneasy feeling then and thought it may be prudent if Alan accompanied us up the stairs, but on reaching the bedroom, sure enough we could see a large chimpanzee gently swinging in the tree. At least it was a very good resemblance of one but in fact was a black dustbin bag deposited there by the wind. We had a good laugh over the episode and left our caller rather shamefaced and very apologetic.

One of the sections in the zoo was known as Whipsnade, named after the zoo in Bedfordshire, because they were both created in the same year. At that particular time the Whipsnade section was responsible for the meat store and supplying the meat rations around the zoo for the various carnivores. They were a little behind one morning and one of the other sections had not had their allocation of meat and making a call via the switchboard to an unfamiliar operator, asked to be put through to Whipsnade. The zoo in Bedfordshire was rather surprised when an irate Chester keeper wanted to know where his b...... meat was, and how long it was going to be before he got it.

I used to get a number of calls offering food for the animals and a surprising number of these came from fish suppliers who had been left with a consignment of fish not good enough for people but alright for the animals, as they put it. I had to explain that if it wasn't good enough for us to eat then I wouldn't dream of feeding it to our stock. It was the same with fruit, although in the autumn we used to get a quantity offered from people who did not want the produce from their trees. We were grateful to accept these provided they were a sweet variety as it was normal for us to purchase in the region of three quarters of a ton of apples weekly as part of the animal rations.

Being the leading zoo in the area, we were usually contacted in the event of identified or unidentified animals being reported. Although many of these calls appeared to be legitimate and the callers genuinely thinking they had seen something out of the ordinary, it was rare to be able to confirm it.

A full turn out one day to catch an escaped lion on a railway embankment turned out to be nothing more than a chase after a rather fat golden Labrador.

I was called out to investigate a so called puma's footprints that had been left by an animal feeding on a sheep carcase only to find that they had been made by a dog, and not a big one either.

A beast supposedly terrorising another country area having been "identified" by locals as a black panther was correctly identified as a large black Great Dane.

Another black panther was seen on a number of occasions over a short period in another area and then was never heard of again, as far as I was aware.

I am convinced that because one supposed sighting gets a bit of publicity, other people then begin to suspect they see something and immediately tie it in with what they have heard, and the rumour spreads. But the following happened in good light and was seen by two perfectly sane people at the same time, and was something for which I can offer no explanation.

The two witnesses were out horse riding near Altrincham, and on rounding a corner on a country road were amazed to see two tigers walk down the road in front of them and turn into a small wood going out of their sight. I questioned them on the reaction of the horses, but apparently there wasn't any adverse effect on them at all and I could only assume that both had seen some sort of apparition, because I was certain there would have been some response if the horses had seen a big cat. I suggested that sunrays coming through the trees may have played a trick on their eyes but both were sure tigers were what they had seen. I also said if there were tigers loose in the area they would be certainly have attracted far more attention. Being carnivorous they would also require quite an amount of meat which would not be supplied by the local butcher and a few people would have been complaining about losing stock. I am not at all sure I convinced them, but have never heard another word about tigers in Altrincham.

Yes, Mr Bell has to be congratulated on his invention, but I also feel he has something to answer for.

Chapter 10

"Problems with plants"

Besides the well known collection of animals, Chester Zoo is renowned for its plants and well tended flower beds carefully nurtured by the gardening staff, who being rightly proud of the displays created, did not always see eye to eye with the keepers whose charges were more likely to view the plant exhibits as just another food item when given the opportunity.

Although it was a rare occurrence to have escapes from the enclosures, it did happen from time to time, and when it did and we found the animal where it should not be, more often than not it involved the gardens.

Bubbles, the African elephant bull, was one of the larger animals to cause a little friction between the keepers and the gardeners. Inside the elephant house down the public passage were a series of hanging baskets containing plants for decoration. The brackets to support the baskets had been placed at a distance estimated to be well beyond the reach of the largest elephant, but regularly, during the evenings, a basket would be stripped of its plants. Obviously the elephants were to blame but the question remained, how were they doing it. A little bit of detective work had to be done, which meant spending a little time after tea, watching, unknown to the occupants. It didn't take too long to catch the guilty party. Bubbles walked to the edge of the enclosure, extended his trunk and gave a hearty blow at the basket, which suspended on its chain, started to swing to and fro. Two or three huge puffs were sufficient to bring the basket closer and closer to his trunk, and it then became a formality to grab a plant as it came within reach for a well earned titbit. I did suggest that planting them with turnips may be the answer, but my advice was turned down in favour of extending the brackets a few feet to take them well beyond reach, which solved that particular problem. I formed the opinion that Bubbles was quite aware of what he was doing and also that he knew he shouldn't do it, because he never once attempted to reach the forbidden fruit during the day, when he could have been seen by the keepers.

Some of the elephants were also very adept at stealing a rose or two from the border surrounding their outside enclosure. Once the green leaves started to appear in the spring those and the flowers that followed were considered fair game. They would position themselves carefully, and gradually ease their bodies over the wall towards the bushes, at the same time transferring weight to stop them overbalancing into the moat. It was a constant battle between the gardeners who tried to prune the bushes so they couldn't be reached, and the elephants who also wanted to prune them and kept trying to reach a little further to do so.

We did have a few accidental escapes over the years and one of the most serious involved a tiger. Early one morning a high wind broke a large branch off a tree beside the tiger enclosure, and this fell across the high wire mesh fence, creating a gap through which an inquisitive tigress wandered for a look at the outside world. Fortunately it was too early in the morning for visitors so we had the zoo to ourselves. The male probably not quite so curious as his mate and still in the paddock, was quickly enticed into the inside quarters and fastened in. It was then the female's turn. She had not gone far apparently, not finding liberty too exciting, she had just wandered round the corner and flattened herself in a bed of wallflowers surrounding the paddock. She looked quite comfortable amongst the flowers and remarkably well camouflaged when suddenly a gardener appeared and got extremely shirty because this animal had the audacity to sit on his flowers. I half expected him to chase it away with his hoe, but then discretion proved to be a little stronger than valour and we were allowed to get on with the task of returning her to the enclosure. As we have noticed on a few occasions when an animal has escaped, they are not happy at being away from their own territory, and the tigress seemed rather pleased to find her way back through the gap when pointed in the right direction, and gently persuaded by some weld-mesh panels.

Another animal suffering some verbal abuse was a female chimpanzee who had crossed a water barrier and had the effrontery to run across a flower bed containing a colourful array of polyanthus. She was severely admonished by one of the gardeners for doing it, but on doubling back and again crossing the border; the voice and its owner rapidly disappeared through a convenient door and took no further part in the proceedings. The chimp continued on her way and entered a nearby ladies loo, by which time we were close on the trail but then had to stop and shout loudly, having no wish to see anything embarrassing. We need not have worried; the chimp had emptied the building far quicker than we could have done.

The parrot house was the home of a pair of Kea, a New Zealand bird which must be a strong candidate for the comedian of the parrot family. A shepherd friend of mine who had worked among sheep for a time in New Zealand, told me of a number of tricks that he had seen the wild parrots do including using the corrugated roof of his shed as a slide. He told me they would continually fly up to the top and slide down again creating a terrific din inside. Having heard his tales I wasn't too surprised at the tricks ours got up to.

Early one morning, one of the pair escaped and made its way to a nearby flower bed where it nipped off all the heads of the French Marigolds planted round the border, and laid each one in a neat row round the bed. Not believing a mere bird could be capable of such a deed a keeper caught the full force of a gardener's wrath for being the vandal responsible.

The beavers regularly made a break for freedom by building "dams" against the walls of their enclosure in the middle of the zoo. These had to be dismantled daily before they got too large and enable the beavers to climb over. One beaver, proving very diligent, managed to reach the top one night and dropped over the wall, the direction then taken plainly obvious by the presence of muddy footprints leading towards the zoo's canal system. We subsequently found it there later in the morning looking quite snug in its new surroundings and decided to leave it at liberty so long as it did no damage to the gardening exhibits, and it also gave the passengers on the pleasure boats something else to look for. For a number of days it seemed quite happy to exist on its normal diet of fruit and vegetables put out for it on the little island that it had decided was a good place to make its home. Then one night it reverted to nature and chewed through the trunk of the director's favourite ornamental willow tree. Any other common willow may have gone unnoticed, but a single tree situated on a small island in the middle of a lake and now laying on its side was rather obvious, so orders arrived to catch the offending animal. Probably realising its mistake it had already got the message and disappeared on its own accord from the zoos premises. It had found its way across a couple of fields and into the Shropshire Union Canal and the next thing we heard, had arrived at Ellesmere Port about five miles distant down the canal, and was now swimming around the Boat Museum.

A rally had been organised for the following day at the museum and when we arrived with our catching equipment, preparations were well under way. Plenty of interested spectators led us to the side of a newly restored Chinese Junk where we found our quarry busy beavering away on the waterline. After a few attempts to catch it in a large net, which came to nothing, we decided to leave it until the following morning as the light was quickly fading. Fortunately beavers are not noted for their intelligence and are quite easy to catch in a trap, and we had brought one with us just in case it was needed. This trap consisted of a large wire cage with an automatic door which closes when an unsuspecting animal enters to sample the bait. This was set on a floating platform baited with a selection of the beaver's favourite fruits including bananas which I knew it would find hard to resist and left at the side of the junk, an area which it had appeared to adopt for the time being. When we arrived early the following morning, it was soon evident from the cheers of other early risers, that we had been successful and found our beaver sitting happily in the crate, replete on the meal left for it and patiently waiting to be collected. We left maybe just a little hurriedly in the hope that there were no holes or permanent damage in any of the boats, certainly none appeared to be sinking and none of the owners were shaking their fists at us, and some even gave a cheery wave for the bit of unexpected entertainment as we headed for home.

Two capybara were released one night by an intruder and were quickly missed the following morning, when a search soon revealed one swimming in the chimpanzee moat. It was soon apprehended and returned to its proper place of residence but the other could not be found anywhere, and nothing was heard of it until about three weeks later. We then had a definite report from one of our junior members, who had spotted it in a field about three miles from the zoo. It seemed to have followed the same course as the beaver for some distance and then left the canal in preference for one of the drainage ditches in the area. I took David, one of the keepers, and the usual catching equipment in anticipation of catching the absconder, and after getting permission from the farmer, we arrived at the field where it had been seen. Full of hope that it would still be in the vicinity, we began a search of the area. A tractor driver, engaged in some field work, was asked if by any chance he had seen the capybara about, but from the blank expression I received, it was obvious he had no idea what I was talking about. I then described the animal in rather more detail and a wide smile arrived on his face. *"Oh that,"* he said. *"It's been here weeks. I thought it was an otter, it lives in that culvert under the motorway."*

Now we had a good idea where it was and where to look, a net was set up at the entrance to the culvert and David, more mobile than me, volunteered to walk down the tunnel which would have been a much simpler task if he had been nearer the size of the capybara. About two minutes later an excited expletive came echoing towards me, which indicated they had met, in fact it had run between his legs, upending him, and was now rushing towards me sounding more like a charging rhinoceros than a capybara in the confines of the culvert. The net however, did the job perfectly and we were soon on the way home, errand successfully completed, much wetter and dirtier than when we had arrived, but at least having the satisfaction of knowing that one person should now be able to recognise a capybara the next time he saw one, even if he may not recognise an otter.

The meerkats were much more subtle; they constructed a burrow from their enclosure to an escape hole concealed under a bush in a small adjoining shrubbery. Reports of meerkats foraging for food on a picnic lawn were discounted for quite a while because none were ever found missing from their cage whenever a count was made. It was only when a keeper spotted one and gave chase only to see it disappear under the bush and reappear seconds later in the enclosure, that their enterprising scheme was brought to an end.

A peacock was not so lucky and came to a sticky end. I would have liked to see these stately birds loose in the grounds, and tried to persuade our gardeners that they would do far more good than harm by clearing up many of the insect pests, but they were insistent that they would scratch the plants up and have dust baths in the flower beds and borders.

We used to clip the feathers on one wing of each peacock annually to stop them flying and keep them on the paddocks. One must have been missed, because one day it took wing and had a good look round the zoo before alighting on the high fence surrounding the tiger paddock. Then unfortunately it made the wrong decision and hopped down on the wrong side. The tigers, not animals to miss an opportunity like that, thought it was suddenly Christmas having such a delicacy as a peacock present itself, and gave the poor bird no chance to fly out again.

But of course the problem was not all one sided, in the friendly conflict between gardens and animals, as having disposed of the plant life, the animals had an end product which was most desirable to put beneath the plants, and the only complaint I heard about that was the fact that the gardeners had to dig it in.

Chapter 11

"Some more dogs"

We had been at Chester for a year and the children had made new friends and found more pets. We still had Rocky with his mumblings about another world and the impressions of laying hens now, plus a new vocabulary of English words which almost gave him the ability to have an intelligent conversation with you. *'Good morning,'* were the first words uttered as soon as he saw you in the morning, and it was *'Good night,'* as soon as the light went out at night, never in the wrong place, and he was seldom quiet in between. We had extended the collection of tropical fish to include a few more exotic species, which we found far more relaxing to watch, and almost as entertaining as the television. The children had acquired some guinea pigs and not having a granary now, a large pen was constructed on the rear lawn to contain the animals and to a large extent saved pushing the lawn mower up and down. We had a resident tawny owl that used to roost in a large cupressus tree in the garden and was probably attracted by the whistling of the guinea pigs. We had various other things around such as caterpillars and stick insects, and a thriving colony of harvest mice, but we didn't have a dog.

There is probably something in a person's blood that makes him wish to have a dog around. I have been associated with them all my life and not having one at the time, missed their company. Wherever we went, dogs seemed to be attracted to us, or maybe it was the other way round, but I was constantly pestered to find one to join the family.

Juno was the one we found. I thought if we are going to have a dog, then we would have a dog. She was a harlequin Great Dane, two years old; she had a good pedigree, but was not a show dog and surplus to the breeder's needs. The children and I collected her one afternoon when Maveen was out, and also totally unaware of our intention, on her return, her face was a picture, as she was confronted with guinea pigs, husband and three children who were grooming something that resembled a friesian calf in size, sitting on the lawn. Juno was practically white all over with just a few black markings which let her down for breed conformity, but we were wanting her other qualities more. She was just a little nervous when she first joined us, which is to be expected with a new dog, but rapidly settled into our routine and was soon showing the Great Dane breed's qualities as one family dog. She could be a little boisterous at play and surprisingly fast at full gallop. Simon, only two years old at the time, was the most vulnerable to her periodic charges round the garden, but soon learnt to anticipate them by sitting down before he was knocked down. Maxine seemed to develop a special relationship with Juno, probably because she was the one to take her on long walks, although more often than not it was my job to feed her. There were never any real worries about strangers approaching Maxine if the dog was with her. Juno's appearance alone could be quite off-putting, but she also showed another side to her nature one evening.

They were out for a walk together when Maxine met a friend. In way of a greeting, he was just about to pat her on the back and suddenly found his arm in Juno's mouth. He suffered no harm, not even a scratch, but it served as a gentle warning not to try to hit her mistress. She also proved to be a great deterrent to unwelcome travellers, as any strangers at the door were welcomed with a deep gruff bark and a warning growl usually sufficient to let anybody know that it might not be safe to loiter.

Juno also had a gentle side and would accept any animal brought into the house as part of the family, even to Maxine's pet rat, and later her boa constrictor. Given the opportunity, I think she would have tried to mother them. Many people may consider that a large dog like Juno would be always in the way in the house, but we never found that to be the case, in fact I think it was her sheer size that stopped you falling over her. You certainly couldn't miss seeing her and I have found smaller dogs are more likely to get under one's feet. Sadly Great Danes do not enjoy a great longevity, eight or ten years being considered about an average life span.

Juno was ten years old when she started to show signs that her life was coming to an end, and it was then that Genghis came into our life. He had been bred by some breeder friends who had sold him as a puppy and had been well reared, but then had changed hands and been neglected. He came back to our friends in such a state that they thought he would be unlikely to survive, but with careful nursing they brought him round, until his increased virility brought him into direct conflict with their own stud dog, causing problems in the kennels.

**Genghis and Arabian Gazelle Omar,
courtesy of John Doidge.**

They asked us if we would like to have him and we went out to have a look to see really, what he thought of us. We thought Juno was big, but Genghis was huge. He took an immediate liking to Maveen and from then on he was her dog. He was still very thin, resulting from his long illness, but now healthy and just in need of TLC (a term our vet used frequently for tender loving care). Maxine was now married and had left home, and our older son was contemplating the same fate, so we were getting more room for ourselves. We had moved home, had a larger garden without the guinea pigs, and plenty of space for the two dogs. With company of her own kind, Juno actually perked up somewhat and lasted another year before finally almost losing the use of her hind legs, and with much regret was put to sleep. Genghis however, continued to thrive and became more attached to Maveen almost to the point of embarrassment, sitting outside the 'loo' door when the little room was visited, and sleeping outside the bedroom door at night. We then found Genghis had other unsuspected qualities you would not expect in a dog. In my work at the zoo, I often found myself with an orphan baby of one sort or another to feed, and usually these were taken home to make the night feeds an easier operation. The Dane had attributes more likely to be associated with a bitch than a dog where the baby animals were concerned. Juno had been good, but Genghis could only be described as superb. Whilst he was with us, we had gazelles, tiger cub, monkeys, chimpanzee, pumas, pigs, porcupine and civet in the house, all of which he guarded zealously and a little excited bark, which he saved just for the occasion, told us if anything was amiss with them. He also had another bark which sounded like a rumble of thunder, saved for anybody who had the temerity to ring the front door bell, something he never failed to hear even if we did. Taking him for a walk was rather like exercising a small pony, and you could sense a feeling of uneasiness in some people meeting him for the first time, not without good reason, because his head was chest high compared with a normal person.

I have yet to come across a dog that does not like to ride in a car, every one that I have had has enjoyed the experience and Genghis was no exception. The only problem with him was when he got on to the back seat there was no room for anyone else and he used to slobber all over the windows. He also had one more drawback and that was his tail. If he was excited he would hit you with it, when it was wagging, you knew you had been hit and it could reach quite a distance to do it.

I would like to think Genghis enjoyed his life with us;

we certainly enjoyed having him and his company. There is something indefinable about a Great Dane that no other breed seems to possess and the sense of security he gave was greatly missed, especially by Maveen when, after a short illness, we lost him at the good age of ten years.

It was quite some time before we could consider another dog after Genghis, but then we succumbed once again. By now retirement was looming and another dog would be with us for a long time, so that had to be taken into consideration. With that in mind, we went from the sublime to the ridiculous. A local breeder had a litter of miniature dachshunds and being somewhat impressed by one owned by a friend, we decided that we would have one. It was rather like starting a family again. Sherry, as we called her, wasn't exactly spoilt but seemed to get quite a lot of attention and I thought was getting rather too possessive for her own good. It was then we found a three-year old bitch of the same breed looking for a good home, so she became a companion for Sherry. I don't think we could have chosen two better dogs to take my wife and me into retirement, they are ideal companions for each other and visitors find it hard to tell them apart. Sherry is Maveen's dog and Chrissie is mine, and that is the way they sorted themselves out without any encouragement from us.

Chapter 12

"They came for dinner and stayed for tea"

Way back in my days on the farms it was not unusual to have a succession of baby animals being fed on the bottle. In my early days it was essential to rear as many animals as possible, as loss of life meant less profit for the business, and nobody liked to see an unnecessary death. Therefore, any lamb or piglet orphaned or for some reason unable to be fed by its mother was bottle fed in an attempt to keep them going. Frequently in the lambing season, a triplet lamb or an orphan could be mothered on to a ewe that had lost her own lamb, various means of persuasion often being necessary to get her to accept it as her own. I used to find leaving a sheepdog close to the pen holding the ewe where she could see it usually paid dividends, as the maternal instinct normally would make her protective towards the lamb. Fly was extremely good at this chore and would be quite happy to sit around all day so long as she could see the sheep.

Especially early in the season it was not unusual to find a number of lambs suffering from hypothermia, having been born in the cold conditions, and a method I used then to revive them came in very useful when similar cases were experienced at the zoo.

New born lambs found suffering from exposure in the cold weather were immersed in hot water, as hot as the hand could bear, until the body temperature had returned somewhere near normal, the treatment sounds rather extreme but worked wonders and seldom failed to produce results. Once warmed and dried, the lamb was always ready to take milk from the bottle. The biggest problem in the early days of this treatment was drying the lamb after getting it thoroughly wet in the bath, towels and a hair dryer were the main tools, and probably the stimulus of rubbing the little bodies helped to revive them during the operation. Later, with the appearance of the ubiquitous plastic bag, it was found that the animal could be put inside the waterproof covering before being given the hot water treatment and much of the drying process was eliminated.

When I moved to the zoo, although it was the practice of some collections to hand rear some of the animals for publicity purposes, we had a policy not to be bottle feed unless there was a genuine reason for doing so. The main cases were complete abandonment by the parent or a lack of milk or some other inability to feed the infant by herself. I have always held the opinion that any young animal large or small should be given the chance to live once it has been born and over the years tried to give them that right.

One of the first of the many zoo babies that spent the first part of their lives in our living room was a polar bear cub. I was passing the bear pool with their keeper one morning and we were amazed to see a newly born cub floating on the surface of the water. Initially we both thought that it was a soft toy dropped the night before by some young visitor, but then realised it was alive when a light movement was seen. It was assumed that it had been born in the water or more likely born inside the den, carried out and left by the mother, but either way it was the only one we could see. The baby was immediately retrieved with a net we had handy to clear litter from the pool and found to be alive, if only just. I took the cub home and gave it to my wife, who having served her apprenticeship with lambs and piglets seemed to be the best foster mum at the time, and told her to forget the housework and concentrate on the cub. Considering the size of a polar bear, the cub must be the smallest baby in comparison to the adult in the animal world, mother weighing in at somewhere around eight hundred pounds, and the weight of the baby not much more than a pound and no larger than a Labrador puppy.

The first objective was to get the cub warmed through and then get some food into it. He, it was a male, was obviously new born having a fresh umbilical cord still attached, and was quickly revived using the tried and tested hot water treatment, and by evening was taking a little diluted milk. As the hours went by it gradually appeared to get stronger, all systems were working and we were getting more confident of success. But this time it was not to be, as after about four days the cub suddenly developed pneumonia most likely caused by the cold water dipping at birth, and died shortly afterwards.

The next baby was one of the rare Arabian gazelles; it had been born during the night and found in a collapsed state suffering from hypothermia the following morning. It was a male and I wasn't very confident that it would survive, but took it home where Maveen put it in a plastic bag and immersed it up to the neck in hot water. It was a little daunting to handle, as its legs looked so thin and delicate; we were frightened they would snap. In no time and as if by magic, the heat and a good rubbing down did the trick and the little calf was standing unaided and searching for a teat to drink from. When I went back over to the section and told the keeper it was standing and furthermore drinking milk, he found it difficult to believe that after being in the condition he had found it, it was possible that it could have survived.

The kennel for the gazelle was a large cardboard box

over which was placed an infra-red pig lamp for heat and it had a towel over a sheet of plastic to lay on. Later, a little hay was added for the bed and also in readiness for when it started to eat solids, which was expected to be at about three weeks of age. From day one, his diet was cow's milk diluted with boiled water, the water part being gradually reduced until the milk was full strength. It was fed six times during the twenty-four hour period, taking about 3oz. at a time initially and eventually cutting the feeds to four a day and increasing the quantity to about 8oz. The young gazelle, named Sultan, was in fact eating solid food by the fourteenth day, in the form of porridge oats. It was at this stage that he was allowed to follow us into the garden and we were a little alarmed when he started to eat soil rather than the more succulent grass on the lawn. The worry was unfounded as it did no harm and later the habit was copied by all the other seven gazelles we subsequently reared, using exactly the same methods, and also assumed eating soil was perfectly natural and possibly was a source of essential minerals and trace elements. It also brought back memories of my grandmother and her assertion that everyone should have the peck of muck, some of these old people probably knew more than they were given credit for.

Although as previously mentioned, a cardboard box was used to confine the gazelles, they were allowed freedom to run around the living room and beyond whenever we were present, and the carpet could have told a few tales about the accidents on it, but then it was found relatively easy to potty train them. As soon as they had finished their bottle, a piece of cotton wool soaked in warm water and wiped under their tail, simulating a mother gazelle washing them, was sufficient to make them defecate and urinate which was then caught, as it happened, in a strategically placed receptacle. This procedure was thought of as quite hilarious by some of our friends and also during visits by various photographers wanting unusual pictures, but saved no end of cleaning up.

Peter, Maveen & Simon with two hand reared Arabian gazelles, Farah and Sultan, courtesy of John Doidge.

We tried to give the gazelles appropriate sounding names and Farah, Omar, Salome, Yasmin, Tabatha, Soraya and Abdul followed in Sultan's footsteps around the house and garden at different times. Although all being from the same species there was a vast difference in their individual behaviour, some would be really confident and inquisitive, others would come and lie at your feet, whilst another would go and lie in the furthest corner, yet all were friendly, and with you just as soon as a bottle of milk appeared. Once strong enough to do so, all the young gazelles would enjoy a gallop round the garden and experiment on the various plants to see which had the best taste.

Whenever we had baby animals in the house, they

seemed to attract press photographers and television cameras, and we had a regular stream to record the event. One afternoon, a television cameraman came to film one of the young gazelles and as usual on these occasions wanted to know what it did. I got the impression with some of the pressmen, they would like you to say, *"Oh, it wears a funny hat and rides a bicycle,"* or something similar. This time some action film was needed, and as it was a nice sunny day I suggested we should go out into the garden where, if it performed as usual, it would lap the house at something like fifty miles an hour. Having set the camera up on the lawn at the front of the house, he said I could let the gazelle go free. When I said I already had and it had passed him three times already, he came to the conclusion it would be better to wait until a little more energy had been expended. Eventually that did happen and some excellent film was obtained of it in a flower bed, eating the roses.

We had Pedro and Pancho together for some of the time, both, as you may guess from their names, as having their family origins in South America. Pedro came first, he was a kinkajou found in his parent's enclosure one morning, clearly abandoned there by his mother. The only reference I could find on hand rearing kinkajous wasn't really helpful or conclusive, as the one in question had died at six weeks old, so we decided to play it by ear. The baby was given the usual warm bath to raise its body temperature and afterwards kept warm on a heater pad. It was fed every two hours initially, with two parts cows milk to one part boiled water, gradually decreasing the water until he was taking full strength milk. He weighed a little under seven ounces at birth which had increased to twelve ounces in two weeks, by which time he was drinking about fifteen mls of milk at each feed, at intervals of three hours. He was also cutting his teeth, and his eyes were open and quite aware of things going on about him. At a month old he was eating some solid food, and soon after that able to walk about, and was then weaned off his bottle at nine weeks, though still taking a quantity of milk by lapping.

Like all our house guests, Pedro wasn't confined and was allowed to wander through the house, which we found wasn't the best of ideas as he grew. Being naturally nocturnal, he would prefer to sleep in daylight hours and do his foraging at night, and for the last few weeks in our care we had to leave him in his large cage after we had gone to bed, and let him exercise when we were around to save any further breakages.

Pancho was a viscacha, the first to be born at the zoo, and arrived about two weeks after Pedro. He was found during the keeper's early morning round, looking more dead than alive. When I took him home, Maveen wanted to know what the smell was, and if it was going to continue smelling like that, she wanted nothing to do with it. I had to agree the stench was rather obnoxious and said the male in the enclosure could be responsible, and probably marked the baby by urinating over it as its fur was wet and sticky, but once it was cleaned up it should be fine.

When he had been revived the youngster became very alert and also quite vocal, he was well developed and looking rather like a large version of a baby guinea pig. He quickly learnt to drink milk from an eye dropper, and as the kinkajou was being fed at three hourly intervals, he followed the same routine, being fed at the same time and using the same milk. He began eating solids at four days and by now was smelling much sweeter. Closely related to a chinchilla but much larger Pancho grew quickly and became very active, going everywhere just as fast as his legs would carry him, usually accompanied by noises resembling atmospherics on a faulty radio and frequently taking a leap into the air, and taking off again at full speed in whichever direction he was facing when he came back to earth. He also had a habit of nipping with his large incisor teeth when he wanted something, which did cause keepers to worry somewhat when he eventually returned to the collection, especially when the nip was accompanied by some of his peculiar utterings. We actually became quite proficient at recognising the sounds he made and could tell what he was wanting by the different tones emitted.

Another rodent reared was Pickles, an African porcupine. She was the sole survivor of a litter of three, and just like a smaller edition of her parents. Like many other babies that we had, we had her in a large cardboard box with a heater pad inside. Boxes were readily available from our stores department and seemed to give the occupants a sense of security; they were warm and draught proof and could be disposed of when soiled.

When still small, Pickles seemed to prefer dark places and would try to hide away after having her feeds which were similar to those of the viscacha. By accident one time, she found my trouser leg afforded the security she craved and disappeared accordingly. She managed to gain access on a few occasions in different trouser legs after that and make progress upwards. After the first time I was careful to make certain it didn't happen to me again. The problem was her spines prevented her from reversing, so the progress was always upwards, and we had a few laughs at the expense of our friends. I often thought it was a wonder that we had any. When Pickles, Prickles may have been more appropriate, was large enough to return to the collection, all the section keepers thought it marvellous to have such a friendly porcupine to show our visitors, a species not really renowned for their amiability.

Rearing Pancho and Pickles gave me an entirely new

insight into the rodent family, though maybe after living with Harold the hare, and having Maxine's pet rat around, I shouldn't have been too surprised. After having both at such a close proximity I had learnt quite a lot from them, and was constantly surprised at their intelligence and ability to make their wishes known, and I had a higher regard for the whole family.

We then acquired our first marsupial. We had quite a large group of Bennetts wallaby in the collection and Wally, as he became known, was picked up on the paddock having been ejected from his mothers pouch, probably in the early morning, as although the small body was cold, there were still signs of life.

At birth a young wallaby is about an inch long, weighing about the same as a sugar lump and having been born then has to find its way into the mothers pouch, a journey for the small embryo of some six to eight inches. Once there it attaches onto a milk gland which swells slightly inside the babies' mouth and normally, it would not relinquish hold until it is covered by hair and ready to put an appearance into the outside world. As it was impractical to catch the wallabies one by one to search which had lost a baby and time was of the essence, Wally was taken home. He was about four inches long discounting his tail, naked and eyes still tightly closed, and I left him with Maveen asking her to do whatever she could for him, as I was in rather a hurry. I did not have great expectations as I went home at lunchtime, fully expecting her to say it was dead, but she had managed to revive it be getting the body heat up, and also to give it a spot of milk with an eye dropper. By evening the little wallaby was getting stronger so we decided to see if we could manufacture a pouch to keep him in, as near as possible a replica of its mother's. I had just purchased a wash leather to clean the car and that appeared to be ideal material, so it was shaped into a bag by a bit of clever needlework, suspended inside an ever present cardboard box and placed under a pig lamp to maintain the necessary heat. Some lanolin was smeared inside the pouch, and a little also rubbed on the infant wallaby, to stop the skin getting too dry. This became home number one and although it looked a little "Heath Robinson" worked admirably. In the evenings home number two was generally down my shirt front, as the baby was fed every hour for a start and it usually took about half an hour to get it satisfied, thus saving me getting up and down to collect from home number one every time he was due. We found it didn't suckle like most mammal babies and relied more on being force fed, and as it couldn't take more than a small drop at a time, the early feeds took quite a while. As he grew, for a small animal he had an enormous appetite and his day was occupied be three things, eating, sleeping and getting into mischief. He did do me one good turn however. I had been looking for an acceptable method of deterring other people's cats from using the soft soil in my garden for what they should have been doing in their own, and when Wally was out in the garden grazing, he absolutely terrorised them. I don't know whether they mistook him for some giant rat but they didn't return after tangling with him.

Wally never lost his liking for human company whilst we had him at home and seemed to possess an instinctive passion to find sanctuary in any equivalent of a pouch. Most times a handy sweater would do, and many of our friends would be suddenly surprised when they sat down to find Wally disappearing up the front of the first skirt or jumper he arrived at. Wally was another great character we missed considerably when it was his turn to go back and join the others of his own kind in the collection. It was a move he took in his stride, and although always one of the friendly wallabies he never appeared to miss being a house guest.

Tiger cub Ranee, courtesy of John Doidge.

Ranee had to be one of our favourites. She was a tiger cub born one Saturday morning just as I was preparing to have a week's holiday. The cub was one of four born in the first litter of one of our females, all of which were scattered around and at first glance appeared to be dead. As they were picked up by the keeper he detected a slight movement in one so I decided there and then to give it a chance of survival. As I walked through the door at home with the pathetic bundle wrapped in a towel, Maveen asked what I had brought, and on being told, wondered what we were going to do with it. I said if it was still with us on Monday morning it surely wouldn't mind having a holiday with us, and after the weekend it did just that. As soon as the cub was revived, using the tried and tested hot water method, she began crying quite lustily and was soon taking some milk. Although there was a cat milk substitute on the market I didn't have any to hand, so again relied on cows' milk which apart from being easy to obtain was always consistent something not easy to achieve when mixing very small quantities of powder. I firmly believe that cows' milk, as bought on the doorstep, contains most of the essential ingredients the majority of mammal babies required, but I also used a child's vitamin and mineral supplement in conjunction with it on all the young animals I reared, and continued to use the same on the tiger cub. I am also convinced that bodily contact and heat are equally important to successfully rear them. Ranee's bright blue eyes, which eventually turned brown, had opened before we returned from our few days rest at the end of the week, and was noticeably putting on weight. After three weeks she was quite strong on her legs and beginning to eat pieces of shredded meat and chicken, fed raw. We didn't have any real problem rearing Ranee, although a certain amount of hair loss was experienced on her neck and shoulders which I put down maybe to some deficiency in the milk, or maybe holding her in that area whilst giving her a bottle. Whichever, I never knew for certain but it quickly grew again once she started eating solid food. It was a completely new experience having a tiger in the house and as she grew, proved to be a worthy adversary for Genghis. Although Ranee played hard and loved a good rough and tumble she could also be very gentle, and never broke skin with tooth or claw. We found we could even let our young grandson, then about a year old, play with her on the carpet. He used to poke fingers in her eyes and ears but she never retaliated, seeming to know that she hadn't to play rough like she could with adult members of the family. She also loved to ride in the car, maybe associating it with the first traumatic week of her life. Picking up the car keys was a signal to her that there was a chance of a ride coming up, and she would try her best to get outside and into the car as soon as the door was opened, and once inside it was a job to get her out before she had her ride. Her favourite position was on the back window ledge, probably because Genghis had already commandeered the back seat, and with a tiger in that position we got more than our share of odd looks. We were extremely sorry when it was time for Ranee to go back into the zoo, we had probably kept her a little longer than had really been necessary, and as she was almost the size of a Labrador dog we were beginning to get a little worried in case she was tempted to chase one as it passed the garden gate, but up to then had shown no tendency to do so. Fortunately with Ranee, as well as the other orphan babies, I could still see them daily once they returned to the zoo, so the break was not quite so hard. Being so tame they all came in for a little extra attention from the keepers and maybe did not miss our attentions quite so much.

A female Brazilian tapir, one of the many born at Chester, did not appear to be thriving soon after being born and a check on the mother showed that her milk had dried up, so Suki had the distinction of being the largest zoo baby we had in the house. It was a bit of a fight to get her to drink initially, having suckled from her mother I think she was a little reluctant to change, but once the situation was mastered she could empty a bottle in record time, and again I used cows milk as the substitute feed. Genghis, who was marvellous with our lodgers, seemed to be more put out with Suki who, once she had settled in began to push him around and usually ended up in prime position in front of the fire, much to the dog's disgust. Suki didn't stay long with us at home. When she was three weeks old she was well onto solid food and had increased so much in weight and size, she was able to go back and delight our visitors and still enjoy her bottles of milk, though now given by her keeper.

Genghis the Great Dane with puma cubs, Elsa and Elsie.

Two puma cubs were next in line and it was quite a treat having two of the same species together at the same time. Even so, in the past we had found that even natural enemies could be the best of friends when they were young. Ranee the tiger used to have great games with a gazelle and it was never really clear who was chasing who round the garden, especially when the dog joined in, and there was never any malice shown by any one animal to the others.

The two pumas were reared using the same formula as Ranee, that of cows' milk and vitamin supplement. I could see no reason in changing a successful method, though new substitute feeds for most species were appearing on the market. They were eating meat and chicken at four weeks which unfortunately had the effect of making them smell quite strong, something which was not so noticeable with the tiger cub. I must admit Maveen was not particularly sorry when they were returned back to keeper care, by which time they had reached about ten weeks old and had become extremely attractive animals.

It was early December when we got Pip. He was a baby squirrel monkey found on the floor of his cage during the morning check, and it was obvious his mother had no milk to feed him and furthermore did not want anything to do with him, so he became our first monkey guest. Once again, I did not forsake the usual formula with which I had success many times, although there were the many recognised milk substitutes. I was now convinced that if a diet is started, unless there are obvious adverse effects, it is far better not to change for another milk or substitute, and there was certainly no cause to change this particular diet with Pip.

He became Maveen's pet, for want of a better term, and she could hardly do anything without him wanting to be involved at the same time. Strangely, I have noticed on a number of occasions that a male animal is more inclined to go for a lady's company, whereas a female animal would prefer a man's, and this has happened with a variety of animal species.

Pip the squirrel monkey, courtesy of John Doidge

About the only thing Pip did not like was water, and I think that was attributable to the fact that one evening he wandered off upstairs whilst I was preparing a bath and jumped in before he realised that water was wet! Luckily the water was warm, but it was sometime before he ventured upstairs again after that episode, which perhaps was not a bad thing. He also had a fetish about examining teeth, most of our friends having to undergo the experience of having their mouths opened, followed by Pip's investigation. We had him for nine months and the return to his family was rather extraordinary. When he was reintroduced to the family cage, only two monkeys moved, Pip and his mother meeting on the ground in the centre of the cage. They had not seen one another since the day he was born, yet appeared to recognise the common bond between them and were inseparable companions afterwards.

I have purposely left Gemma till last, as she was our favourite amongst the many infants we reared. I couldn't keep count of the number of times I have been asked which is your favourite animal, a question I usually answer with, *"I don't have favourites, I like them all,"* but there were a number that have left their mark and I will never forget. Gemma, she was one of those unforgettable animals.

She was a female chimpanzee and being one of our closest relatives in the animal world I suppose it was inevitable she would be treated as "almost human". She weighed just three pounds and one ounce the day she was born and totally ignored by her mother, unfortunately, not an uncommon occurrence. A few baby chimpanzees had already been reared in the collection successfully and there was a recognised diet for them, and a proprietary human baby milk substitute was the one recommended, so that was the one used to rear our new baby.

Chimpanzee Gemma with Tigger the house cat, courtesy of John Doidge.

Gemma was treated exactly the same as a human baby, the recognised way to treat a baby chimp, being fed every three hours which after seven weeks were gradually cut to five daily feeds. She cut her first tooth at ten weeks and her second a week later and like many human babies there were an increased number of dirty nappies during the process. Again like a human child they can be quite trying and do demand that you spend time with them, and I think the more time you can devote to them the easier they are to rear and can also become quite neurotic if left too much on their own.

It requires a year or more of undivided attention before a baby chimp is independent enough to go back into the collection, and then still needs individual care before it can be mixed with the others, although they are far more intelligent and demanding than a human of the same age. Obviously with a baby of this nature you have to be prepared to stay at home during holiday periods, or alternatively have one with relatives who are prepared to put up with peculiar people such as ourselves who are in the habit of taking their work home, and that was what we usually did. On days out or even on the weekly shopping expeditions if the weather was fine and warm, Gemma came with us. She was rather averse to accepting baby sitters and if we did have to go out and leave her, it was advisable to make sure she was well fed, settled down and fast asleep before leaving her with one. If she did wake whilst we were absent and she missed us then, it was likely she would scream loudly until our return and invariably accompany the noise with a very dirty nappy. It was fortunate she was on the best of terms with Genghis, and he in turn was most protective towards her and was quite instrumental in her upbringing. She used to ride on his back like a miniature jockey and could get quite upset if he went missing for any reason. Another friend was Tigger, a large tabby cat that somehow managed to adopt us, and we often used to find them curled up together asleep and the cat would also spend hours washing her.

One occasion when out shopping, Gemma was not unnaturally mistaken for a human baby, and a man was heard to exclaim with some consternation about the amount of hair on that baby's arm. He wasn't made any wiser at that moment.

Later in the year we were invited to a friend's home following their daughter's wedding reception, together with a number of other guests, and Gemma was with us at the time. She was sleeping in her carry cot when we arrived and as she appeared quite peaceful I left her in the lounge, and was soon approached by a lady, a stranger to me, who asked if the baby was mine, having been told by our host that it was. Thinking Gemma may have woken and was needing attention, I said that she was and mischievously agreed when the lady said she adored babies and could she possibly pick it up. Having said yes, I anticipated the scream long before it came. As soon as the blanket covering her was pulled back, Gemma gave her usual welcoming hoot, leapt out of the cot and shot across the room to me. I have since been forgiven for the incident and have become good friends with the lady concerned, and also had a few laughs about it, although she was less than amused at the time.

Maveen used to take Gemma into the zoo regularly to see the other chimpanzees, so it would not come as too much of a surprise when the time came to join them, and she was later left with two other young ones for short periods to learn how to behave as a chimp should, instead of copying our bad habits. Like the rest of our babies, Gemma eventually went for good, but again like others before her, I was in the fortunate position to be able to see her on my daily rounds and keep on the best of terms with her, and like the others, gone but not forgotten.

Chapter 13

Memories

Years ago it must have been far easier to run a zoo. It was a relatively simple matter to acquire a great assortment of animals through dealers in exotic species and without giving any great thought to the species they represented. Visitors too were then quite happy to see a collection put together, whether it was rare or otherwise, just going for a day out. Today, in the majority of zoological collections, the emphasis has shifted to keeping rare and endangered species and attempting to increase their numbers through combined breeding programmes in captive conditions. This unfortunately cannot be done without finance and the costs have to be met by attracting visitors, and at the same time give them an interesting day out and above all good value for the money they spend, if the zoos are to remain in business. Many of the endangered species are not necessarily the most appealing, and even though television and wildlife programmes have helped to create a great interest in their well-being, in all probability they would not draw the crowds without many of the more common animals that are kept to balance the collections, and ensure there is a good comprehensive selection from the animal world to keep everybody interested.

However, we cannot assume that many of the animals we regard as common at present will not be one of the endangered species very soon. Looking round the world today it is very difficult to find one specie of native wildlife that is finding an easy existence and increasing in numbers without protection, unless it is man himself, and it is not only the animals that are dying, the land that is essential for their survival is also disappearing or becoming polluted.

There are some people today, who do not like zoos, but I ask them to consider the alternative. Do we want a world without animals or would we prefer to see them kept alive in comfortable conditions? The answer is not as simple as that but I know that if I was a gazelle, given the chance I would opt for the relative comfort of a good zoo with food and water in plenty without having to be on the watch constantly, twenty four hours a day for predators, poachers, drought and hunger when the food disappears.

We all have a duty to ensure that our wild animals survive and I have seen enough zoos, and the many dedicated people working in them, during the past quarter of a century to realise that they may be the only chance for some of them. There are already numerous species saved from extinction and others that have a good chance of survival thanks to captive breeding. There are a number of different organisations now who claim to be conservationists. Zoos are proving that they are, and I would like to see all the others, anti zoo or otherwise, get together and pool their resources. If their propaganda is correct, they, and all the good zoos are working towards the same ends.

I have enjoyed immensely the years spent at Chester Zoo and am grateful not only to the animals I have known, but also to all my human friends and colleagues who helped those years to pass away only too quickly.

I would like to think that the younger members of my family and their descendants, and indeed everybody else who follow us, will derive as much pleasure from being able to see as many species as I have, and if zoos can play a small part in making it happen then they will justify their existence.

There are many people who find it difficult to get to sleep when they retire for the night and maybe count sheep, in the hope it will help. If I find myself in that position, I can reflect on the many animals I have known. I have never managed to get to the end of the list, and even if I stayed awake all night I doubt if I would.

My friends are remembered for different reasons, and some come to mind quicker than others, but all the memories are treasured and I do not need the hundreds of photographs I have collected over the years to remind me of them.

The many visitors I met at the zoo had their favourites, some preferring the small cuddly animals, some going for the elephants and others for the many in betweens, but few appeared to go overboard for antelopes.

I decided kudu were fun when Charlie and his mate Zoe, were brought out of quarantine and put on a mixed paddock in the zoo, with wildebeest and ostrich for company. Charlie had become very friendly whilst in the close confinement at Prenton and continued in the same vein when he came down to Chester, almost to the point of being cheeky. Completely out of character for an herbivore he developed a taste for chicken. Part of the ostrich diet at the time were some of the unwanted male chickens, sex-linked from a local hatchery which were also used for the birds of prey and the many small carnivores in the collection, and some of these were fed daily to the big birds in the paddock. Charlie was caught one day chasing the ostrich away and helping himself to their food, and he would charge across the paddock afterwards, as soon as the keeper appeared with the ostrich food, demanding a couple of chicks before the birds could be fed, and an imposing sight he was careering across the field.

After coming to the zoo, it wasn't long before Zoe's first calf was born and then immediately abandoned by her. The male calf was rescued, and as being a little too large to take home, was put under a heat lamp in one of the buildings near the time, office and where he was handy to reach from home.

Young male, Kudu Quango, hand reared by Peter.

The calf was called Quango and took to a bottle like a duck taking to water. He was fed on cows' milk, fortunately only requiring one night feed, and grew quickly into a strapping youngster and although we had to be constantly aware of his sharp horns as he was growing, it was unbelievable just how friendly he was, even when he became a mature animal. To rear a wild animal and to have its complete trust returned has a most rewarding feeling and although experienced many times, is one that is hard to describe.

I learnt about Big Red whilst I was working my way around the zoo just after I arrived. He was a large red kangaroo who when standing upright could look you straight in the eye, though he seldom did as he was far too devious. I was warned of his unpredictable nature and told never to turn your back on him as he was apt to attack from behind, clasping his arms around one's neck and then kicking out with his hind legs whilst resting on his thick tail. His keepers tended to be not so forthcoming with new helpers on the section who had to forego the experience of a cuddle and a kick from Big Red. Fortunately the assault was usually more embarrassing than painful for the person concerned.

When I arrived at Chester there were two pairs of rhinoceros, one pair of white and one pair of black, and many visitors would ask why they were identified by colour when it was obvious there was no difference, both being a dirty shade of grey. I soon learnt that the white rhino got its name from the African word 'Wijt' which means broad and referred to the broad square lips of the white species. Being more gregarious in nature than the black rhino, the whites had seldom been bred when kept in pairs and that was maybe the reason ours had not produced offspring. We did, however, have three calves from our other pair, Roger and Susie. Roger was the first rhinoceros bred in a British zoo and born at Bristol, Susie being imported some years before. They were not then appreciated as an endangered species, some 25,000 in existence, but that number is now down to a few hundred. Even so it was a rare occurrence to breed them in captivity and a significant event in the zoos history, and worthy of the press coverage they received at the time. Jasper was the third to be born from our pair and I remember him as being the nearest thing to a miniature animated tank you could get. After being reared, he went to a zoo in the west country and now features in a current breeding programme in the UK. His brother Reginald, went to a somewhat cooler climate, joining a female at Moscow Zoo, some three years earlier.

In my last year at the zoo it was most gratifying to have the fourth baby rhinoceros birth, this time from another pair Esther and Parky, both zoo bred animals and also part of the joint programme. After a couple of days it became apparent that Esthers milk was inadequate and the calf would have to be hand reared. Fortunately this was accomplished with the help of a Vietnamese pot bellied pig. It was a known fact that a baby animal will do better if it has company of some sort, and the nearest thing we had to a baby rhino was the pig languishing in the children's farm. It was a little larger at the time but proved to be a great asset as a companion and was soon dwarfed as the rhino grew, but they still continued to be the best of friends. The young rhinoceros was named Emma, after the daughter of the keeper who had looked after the rhinos in the collection for twenty-five years. She soon became a star attraction featuring in many newspapers and television. Hopefully too, she will become part of the important breeding group and help to keep a rapidly declining species going, for future generations to marvel at.

Boris arrived at the zoo just after I did, he was a young chimpanzee "rescued" from a New York pet shop by the American authoress Hester Mundis. She subsequently wrote a book about him and his early life in her apartment, but like all babies, he grew up and unlike a lot of others not suitable to continue living in a flat, so she had to find him another home. Having visited many zoological collections in her quest to find suitable accommodation and liking the Chester facilities she contacted us and asked if we would be prepared to accept Boris to join our group. Being raised in a human environment he was a friendly animal if somewhat mischievous but soon learnt he was a chimp, when initially put with other hand reared apes of similar age including Rajang, a young orang-utan we had at that time. Boris has since developed into the dominant male in Chester's large chimpanzee group and shows a great deal of intelligence. I do not think he will ever forget his early years when he learnt some human habits and never fails to recognise anybody that he connects with his past, well illustrated when Miss Mundis made a visit to the zoo about twelve years after leaving him in our charge. Boris immediately recognised his foster mother and made more fuss of her than anyone could have expected, and seemed to anticipate that she had brought him some of his favourite chocolate drink before it even came out of her bag. Chester has had an excellent record of keeping chimpanzees recording over seventy births over the years, a number of which are now attributable to Boris. Some of the adults have lived well beyond their expected life span. Babs was one such animal coming to Chester as a youngster just two years old, and then living another forty in the collection. She would always make a fuss when I was on my rounds and I could be sure of a warm welcome from her. She was the one I missed most when she passed away, but I am certain that she did get satisfaction from her long life and the attention given to her from the caring keepers. Possibly due to the more modern keeping methods, when it is tried to simulate a more natural life for the chimpanzees, the young animals appear far more independent, and do not seem to develop into the characters that their parents and grandparents were. Although they all have their own names and vary as much in habit as people, I do not think we will see the likes again of some of those original members of the group such as Algy, Prince, Bolden, Meg and Babs, but Boris is trying his best to live up to that tradition.

It was a great disappointment in 1974 when a long awaited birth of an elephant ended with a stillborn baby, but was however, somewhat compensated three years later with the birth of Jubilee, whose parents were Nobby and Judy. He made history by being the first elephant to survive and be reared in Britain, and in fact only the third to be born, including the previous one at Chester. The other, early in the century, had been conceived prior to its mother being imported in to the country. There are not many elephants born in captivity because the problems of keeping mature bulls and the space required to house them make many zoo directors reluctant to have these potentially dangerous animals in their collections. In the past it was also unnecessary as the young elephants were readily available through dealers, but it was becoming apparent that this system would have to change and zoos would have to breed their own replacements because of declining wild stocks.

I think Chester anticipated this need before many zoos but also probably underestimated all the requirements needed for a breeding group of these large animals. Although we were unaware at the time that Nobby had made Judy pregnant and probably thought him a little young to do so, the female elephants were fully aware of it and following the instincts of a wild herd, decided the male having fulfilled his duties, had no further need to tolerate his attentions.

Nobby was pushed off the island by the two Asian cows who strangely decided the presence of the African bull elephant in the same enclosure posed no threat to their existence. This incident ended in tragedy as Nobby had no intention of returning anywhere near the cows, and despite concerted efforts to bring him under control, he broke though the zoo perimeter fence and there was no alternative but to bring his life to a premature end, as he was then becoming a risk to the public living in the built up area around the zoo. It was the worst event in the zoo's history and a sad loss for everyone concerned.

We had made no preparations for Jubliee's birth as

although the pregnancy was becoming obvious we had no date for the expected birth. Pregnancy testing for elephants was then in its infancy due to the lack of pregnant elephants, and we had sent a blood sample off to a laboratory hoping to help them in their work as well as confirming our suspicions. Not hearing from them a couple of weeks later I rang the laboratory to say we had a very positive result from our independent test, and a calf had been born to prove it.

The young calf was already a few hours old when we came in that morning and moving around confidently. The house however, had a number of hazards that we thought could pose problems for our new baby. There was a deep moat surrounding the enclosure which also contained a capacious bath, and the large African bull was still in attendance. A trailer load of straw bales was quickly spread round the moat to cushion the fall should he drop in and whilst this operation was being completed it became obvious that Bubbles, the bull, was no problem, he was as gentle with the calf as the cows, so the pool became our next priority. Many suggestions were made, filling with sand was turned down because it may fill the drains, filling with straw bales was also a non-starter as it would have been thrown round the house by the elephants, so water was eventually the choice though some were worried he would drown if he fell in. And fall in he did, just as soon as the bath was full. After a few seconds, which seemed like an eternity, he popped up like a cork and was unceremoniously hooked out by his mother. Two more laps of the house and he fell in again, and once again was dragged out by Judy. This display of protective motherhood eased our minds and although he was watched carefully, he wasn't seen to fall in again, though much later quite prepared to walk in and have a good splash around.

Jubilee thrived and so did we, it was one of the rare occasions when the zoo got national media coverage for an animal story, he even got his name from a competition run by the television programme "Blue Peter". I suppose in the Queen's Jubilee year his name was inevitable and even though at the time, many of us though it was not an elephant name, it stuck and now it would be strange to hear him called anything else. The publicity generated by his birth was responsible for an extra one hundred thousand visitors the year he was born, and even now he gets cards sent to him on his birthday from his many fans around the world.

Jubilee was a healthy youngster and apart from the minor scratches and scrapes that every growing youngster manages to get, hardly needed any veterinary treatment. Both cows cared for him, mother Judy being far more strict than auntie Sheba (a very human trait), but also rather like a human baby it was mother he wanted if there was any sign of trouble.

He was 32 inches (81 cms) tall and weighed 210lbs (95kgs) when he was born, and fourteen years later when I retired he stood eight feet tall and weighed over three tons. Jubilee's birth and subsequent survival undoubtedly qualified as the highlight of my life at the zoo.

Hybrid elephant Mottie with mother Sheba, born in Chester, 1978. Jubilee and mother Judy in background born in 1977 (first elephant bred in UK).

In 1978 we had another elephant born, this time the parents were Sheba and Bubbles, and a birth that according to all the genetic experts wasn't possible. It was a hybrid, a cross between the Asian and African species never before seen and probably never to be see again. The elephants and the Chester air had proved that experts can sometimes be wrong, although the sheer incredibility of such a thing happening made the event seem more like a publicity stunt, happen it did, and I do not think it got the attention it deserved in zoological areas. I have found in my experience that it is better not to use the words always and never when describing what animals can and cannot do, because some are sure to prove you wrong.

Mating between Sheba and Bubbles had been observed but none of the dates coincided with the actual birth which when it came took us by surprise, although it was rather noticeable, Sheba could be in a late stage of pregnancy. Our first intimation of the birth came when we had a report from a member of staff, who claimed there was a sea lion on the elephant island being surrounded by the three adult elephants and Jubilee, at about nine thirty in the morning. The sea lion turned out to be our third calf, very small, weak and estimated to be six to eight weeks premature and on examination found to be a male. After several hours he was still unable to stand so we decided to try to get some food into him from a bottle. For the first few feeds he was given glucose and as Sheba had willingly allowed us to take milk from her this was added to cow's milk and vitamin supplement to continue the feeding. Fortunately it was mid summer and quite mild so both Sheba and the calf could be left outside as it was feared that an attempt to move either could have adverse effects. He was never left unattended, and it was midnight on the third day when I came to relieve Ray, one of his keepers, he told me excitedly that "Mottie" as we had called the baby, had managed to stand for the first time and walked a few tottering steps. At two o'clock, he was due for another feed so I went to prepare a bottle and returned a few minutes later to find Mottie had stood up again, and walked straight into the outside pool which had been drained, but still remained wet and muddy in the bottom. He had slipped down and the mud made it difficult for him to get up again and Sheba was in there with him trying to help. The natural light was only sufficient to discern shapes and my torch wasn't a great help, but without giving it much thought I went into the pool to attempt to lift Mottie out, by now wet and slippery. Although Sheba was a gentle animal I did not know how she may react should the youngster cry out in alarm at being manhandled, and she was in very close attendance. Somehow I managed to avoid her trunk and feet, although possibly it was more likely that her trunk and feet avoided me, and between us Mottie was hauled to safety. Lifting something like 160lbs of animated, slippery elephant on a greasy surface is an exercise I would not care to face again, I thought afterwards I probably shouldn't have taken the risk but at the time thought nothing of it. After a warm wash and rub down and a feed, the little elephant wanted to move about and make up for lost time. The following morning the pair were able to walk into the house, and a day later saw Mottie suckling from his mother, and though we were still supplementing his feeds from a bottle, having got the taste for mother's milk we soon found that he was helping himself whenever he felt the urge.

From then on his progress was up and down. He had an infection successfully treated by antibiotics and began to fill out and put on a little weight, but on the eleventh day tragedy struck. We found him lying comatose, and he died within the hour.

Death was caused by a necrotic entero-colitis, in all probability due to a weakness associated with prematurity. The complaint is often symptomless and not uncommon in newly born animals.

In some ways I would have liked to have seen Mottie survive and grow up but it was probably better this way, for him to die in infancy. As a hybrid he could only have been a curiosity and unable to follow the life an elephant should have.

In recent years, Chester has been in the forefront of a plan to get a programme together for breeding elephants in the UK, which hopefully will soon start producing results and also hope that mistakes that were made in the past when gaining knowledge of keeping bull elephants, have now been rectified.

I know that many people are fervently anti zoo; I have met a few travelling around giving talks about my work and have hopefully converted a number of them to my way of thinking, as I hope to continue doing. Of course everybody is entitled to their own opinions but having worked for a quarter of a century in a leading collection, renowned world wide, and having been involved in the work that is going on to prevent many species disappearing forever, I am convinced there is a successful future ahead for good zoos. Fortunately there are also many devoted people I have had the pleasure of meeting and working with during my working life who will strive to ensure as much of our wildlife as possible will survive for future generations to see and marvel at in a rapidly contracting world. I certainly would not have been happy working in a zoo environment and spent that amount of time there had I though otherwise.

Today I am quite happy in my retirement home in north Wales overlooking the Cheshire Plain, the Wirral, Mersey and Dee estuaries, seeing as far as Joderell Bank in one direction and Blackpool Tower in the other, so long as it isn't raining (or going too). My wife and I still share a love of animals and sharing our house are our two miniature dachshunds which at one time just might have been dismissed as lapdogs, but have been pleasantly surprised to find they are excellent little companions and always ready for a romp. Fortunately I don't have to keep up with them when they go for a walk; they exercise themselves in the garden.

I also have a free ticket for the zoo so I can visit whenever I wish and best of all I have my memories of all my friends. Both human and animal.